Systemic Violence
in Education

SUNY Series, Education and Culture:
Critical Factors in the Formation of
Character and Community in American Life

Eugene F. Provenzo, Jr. and Paul Farber, Editors

Systemic Violence in Education

Promise Broken

EDITED BY

Juanita Ross Epp and Ailsa M. Watkinson

State University of New York Press

Published by
State University of New York Press, Albany

For information, address State University of New York Press
State University Plaza, Albany, N.Y., 12246

Production by Diane Ganeles
Marketing by Frank Keneston

Library of Congress Cataloging-in-Publication Data

Systemic violence in education : promise broken / edited by Juanita
Ross Epp and Ailsa M. Watkinson.
     p.   cm. — (SUNY series, education and culture)
   Includes bibliographical references and index.
   ISBN 0-7914-3295-5 (hardcover : alk. paper). — ISBN 0-7914-3296-3
(pbk. : alk. paper)
    1. School violence—Canada—Case studies. 2. School violence—
United States—Case studies. 3. School management and
organization—Case studies. 4. Classroom management—Social
aspects—Case studies. 5. Sexual harassment in education—Case
studies. 6. Schools—Sociological aspects—Case studies. I. Epp,
Juanita Ross. II. Watkinson, Ailsa M. III. Series.
LB3013.3.S97 1997
371.78—DC20
                                      96-36301
                                        CIP
                                        r96

10 9 8 7 6 5 4 3 2 1

This book is dedicated to our husbands,
Walter Epp and Allan Wickstrom,
and to our children, in order of their appearance,
Nathan, Anthony, and Jonathan Epp,
Sheldon, Jeffrey, and David Wickstrom.

We would also like to thank the members of CASWE
(Canadian Association for the Study of Women and Education)
for their input and continued support and Virginia Stead,
for "ever vigilant" research assistance.

Annotated Table of Contents

While students are given "equal access" to an education, disparaging and discriminatory things sometimes happen on the way to graduation and result in reduced student confidence, lowered academic achievement, and high dropout rates. In this chapter, the issues of school culture, school organization, school leadership, and pedagogy are examined for inherently discriminatory and therefore systemically violent patterns.

Authority has traditionally been considered a suitable basis for pedagogy. This gives teachers and administrators tacit permission to use force when it becomes "necessary," that is, when students defy authority and thus compromise their "learning." The applications of authority to pedagogy have strong implications for those who are "other." If we were to seek alternative ways to control children, perhaps women administrators would play a role in changing the way we do schooling.

Teachers and administrators are expected to identify and report incidents of child abuse but this is a complex process which does not always have satisfactory results. Societal bias which accepts male dominance over women and children as the norm, affects the ways in which institutions codify, and sometimes condone forms of child abuse.

Part II: Systemic Violence in Pedagogical Practice

Preschool girls tend to congregate in the art and housekeeping areas and boys engage in more active play with bricks and trucks. How does this happen? An examination of instances in which kindergarten boys appropriate space sheds light on the underlying societal attitudes which allow it to happen.

The simulated worlds of video games can have an impact on the lives and values of young children. This is an ethnographic study of the literacy learning of an English as a second language learner whose life is enmeshed in rule-governed video games and an examination of the violent themes reenvoiced and intertwined throughout the game player's talk, actions, and writing.

Leaving Kenya to study in Canada awakened this author to issues of race, gender, and class, so she chose women's studies courses and other "progressive" programs where there appeared to be a commitment to equity issues. She was to find, for both herself and for her children, that the "house" was far from being clean.

Stories of several people's experiences in the educational system are used to illuminate the dangers of the common educational practice of labeling. When labels and categories reduce living, multidimensional human subjects to lifeless, unidimensional objects they become a form of educational violence.

But labeling is not all bad. This counter argument is added to reflect on the positive aspects of labels.

Part III: Systemic Violence, Women, and Teachers

Teachers who attempt to use student-centered pedagogy find themselves caught in the traps of patriarchy. In attempting to turn away from the "banking" system of rote memorization, teachers find themselves fighting both bureaucracy and the students' romanticized notions of roles and expectations.

Female teachers have learned to live with the sexual harassment they receive from boys. They put up with dirty pictures drawn above their names and whispered sexual slurs. But what would happen if a teacher were to seek institutional support for putting a stop to this insidious violence?

The systemic nature of harassment is sometimes supported by traditional administrative strategies. The "poisoned environment" impacts on learning and undermines the growth and productivity of people and organizations. What do individuals and groups "learn from the learning place?"

When we think about "violence" in our society and in education, we tend to think of violence in purely physical terms. Yet there are far more subtle forms of violence that are just as hurtful, silencing, and damaging. This chapter is an exploration of the kinds of violence three women encountered in their research and in their experiences as teachers and students in educational systems. Their conversations speak to "systemic violence" perpetrated through policies, practices, and structures in educational and social systems.

Part IV: Keeping Promise

This is a personal reflection on how the systemic violence of racism and sexism has affected one person's life and her understanding of what happens when it stops.

Systemic violence in schools is associated with administrative and pedagogical practice. The modification of both would require individual as well as systemic change. In this chapter, we examine the reflections of the book's contributors and integrate their understandings of systemic violence while envisioning a world without it.

Introduction

Systemic violence: Any institutionalized practice or procedure that adversely impacts on disadvantaged individuals or groups by burdening them psychologically, mentally, culturally, spiritually, economically, or physically. It includes practices and procedures that prevent students from learning, thus harming them. This may take the form of conventional policies and practices that foster a climate of violence, or policies and practices that appear to be neutral but result in discriminatory effects.

We spend a great deal of time in schools. In many schools there is a feeling of harmony, but in others there is a disturbing sense of contained anger and authorities seem unaware of the submerged bitterness. Was it our own experiences with abuse of authority that made us angry at smiling concerned officials in staff rooms and in principals' offices? What was it about so many schools that was so disturbing?

Part of the answer was to be found in the liberation pedagogy of critical theory. In abstract forms, Freire (1970), Miller (1990a,b,c), and others explained our problems of dissonance. Miller, in particular, helped us understand how well-meaning people could do abusive things and how school systems could apply "correction" and fail to recognize its cruelties.

We were not alone in our dissonance. At a 1994 conference on violence in schools, many of the papers focused on "zero tolerance" policies as a means to reduce playground battles. But in the women's caucus, the papers took a different turn. Suddenly we were hearing others articulate our dissonance. And they were giving it a name: "systemic violence."

Once we knew its name, we also knew its interconnectedness—in our lives and in the lives of our children. The stories were varied but the themes were constant. In session after session we brought back learnings from the previous hours and pieced together an enveloping picture. In that picture, we found our own stories, observations, impressions, and interpretations. And we knew that unless we spoke out, a similar heritage would be the sentence for our children.

So we set about collecting our experiences and trying to make sense of what we knew. The result is this book. The contributors are a strange collection in that we represent the fusion of theory and practice. Many of us were teachers before we became academics. Some of us are still students or have returned as students after years as teachers. Many of us are mothers reexperiencing education by watching our children from a distance.

Similar to Friedan's "problem with no name" (Friedan, 1993), once we had named our dissonance as systemic violence, we knew its symptoms. The identification became personal as people applied the term to their own experiences: Was it systemic violence when the coach left me sitting on the bench? (Not necessarily). Do you mean like when I wasn't allowed to play ball because I was a girl? (Yes). What about when the teacher embarrassed me in front of the class? (Perhaps). Was it systemic violence when the women portrayed in the English curriculum were exclusively "sex kittens," submissive mothers, or "whores"? (Yes). Was it systemic violence when the principal strapped me? (Yes). How about when the teacher made me stay in to do my homework? (Probably not). Everyone had a story. To determine whether or not a school practice was a form of systemic violence, it was assessed using these questions:

1. Was it violence? That is, did it hurt you or diminish your dignity?

2. Did it prevent you from learning?

These questions are sometimes difficult to answer, perhaps because the systemic nature of the violence makes it seem "normal." In the writings which follow, we will return often to Gramsci's idea of "common sense" (Ng, 1993) in which violent practice seems right and normal because it is so common and so universally accepted.

Our book did not grow in the usual chronological sense. It grew from a convergence of studies and interpretations. While some of us had been collecting thoughts on pedagogy and violence (Epp, chapter 2), others had been reflecting on administrative complicity (Watkinson, chapter 1). Students were learning first hand about discrimination (Ndunda, chapter 6), teachers were reflecting on harassment (Richards, chapter 9; Warren, chapter 10) and confronting misogyny (Whitty, chapter 4; Jadwin, chapter 8; Ho, Webb, and Hughson, chapter 11). Meanwhile, Wason-Ellam (chapter 5) was studying video game violence, Tite was confronting child abuse (chapter 3) and Monteath, Cooper, and Rossler were all wrestling with the labeling of students (chapter 7). It was through coming together at the conference that we realized the connectedness of our topics and our stories.

Defining Systemic Violence

The term *systemic violence* can be deconstructed by seeking to understand each word separately. To begin at the end, *violence* is defined as follows:

> Violence has the effect or potential effect of hurting the health and welfare of an individual. It can be physical, verbal (oral or written), emotional, sexual, or racial, and can be directed against one individual or a group of individuals. Violence can also be expressed as acts of vandalism and damage to property. At the far end of the continuum of violence are criminal acts. However, if we are to reduce violence in schools and in society, incidents at all points along the continuum, even bullying, or continual verbal harassment (e.g., in reference to an individual's disability) can be as debilitating to the victim as a physical attack. If ignored, these incidents can escalate in severity (Ontario Ministry of Education, 1994, p. 12).

Violence is an important issue in schools today, and administrators and policy makers are taking steps to curb what they see as an escalating problem of student defiance and student-to-student violence. *Zero tolerance* has became the watchword of the classrooms, playgrounds, and hallways of our schools.

The original use of the term zero tolerance appeared in a study in response to patient abuse by doctors (McPhedran and Johnson, 1991). It was intended to apply to acts of violence by those who are in positions of authority. The term has since been appropriated by the educational community and the power issues have been reversed. Students who persist in violent actions are barred from schools. Educational applications of zero tolerance do not invite educational decision makers to reflect on the abuse of power against those with less power, which was the term's original intent.

On the surface, the educational application of zero tolerance seems like a positive step. Certainly, few would wish to encourage playground violence, and children who act in violent ways must not be allowed to inflict injury on other children. But such policies do not address the sources of violence. In their summary dismissal of student perpetrators, school authorities do not question causes of violence or the role of the school system in engendering violence. An examination of *systemic* violence shifts the emphasis from the individual student to the system.

Systemic violence is any institutionalized practice or procedure that adversely impacts on disadvantaged individuals or groups. The adverse affects can be seen in psychological, mental, cultural, spiritual, economic, or physical burdens. Thus, institutional or systemic violence can happen in any institution (Government of Canada, 1993). Systemic violence in schools includes those practices and procedures that *prevent students from learning*. The learning environment can be impeded in two ways. It can be impeded by conventional policies and practices that foster a climate of violence (large impersonal schools, the use of corporal punishment) or by those policies and practices that appear neutral on their face but which result in discriminatory effects (Eurocentric bias in curricula, school building design that impedes access).

One of the causes of systemic violence is the assumption of a "norm" that is white, heterosexual, Christian, able-bodied, intelligent, thin, middle-class, English-speaking, and male (Ellsworth, 1994, p. 321). Children who do not fit the norm are adversely affected. Cummins (1989) has noted that students who tend to have the most difficulty in schools are those who have experienced a long history of discrimination, subjugation, and prejudice. But students who fit the "norm" are also harmed by pervasive stereotypical assumptions, and exclusive subject matter and classroom practices that reinforce sexist, racist, elitist, ablist, and heterosexist attitudes (Ellsworth, 1994, p. 306).

The majority of the contributors to this book are Canadians, but the issues raised are international. The list of references, emanating from a wide international collage, is evidence of this. Americans, for example, have debated the issue of school prayer since it was first declared unconstitutional in 1948 (*McCollum v. Board of Education of School District No 71*, 333 U.S. 203, 1948), and presidential candidates still campaign on the issue. Likewise, the use of corporal punishment in schools has been challenged unsuccessfully, all the way to the American Supreme Court (*Ingram v. Wright*, 430 U.S. 651, 1977). Over the past ten years, the number of states prohibiting corporal punishment has increased from four states (Paquet, 1982) to twenty states (Fischer et al., 1991). The *Education of the Handicapped Act*, 1995, and Section 504, *The Rehabilitation Act*, 1973, combine to make the issues surrounding mainstreaming and the misclassification of students some of the most litigated issues in American education. Equality rights are protected in the United States through the *American Bill of Rights* and other federal and state legislation, and in Canada through the *Canadian Charter of Rights and Freedoms*. The issue of inequality in educational results is high on the agenda of educational reformers in many countries (see Kozol, 1991). Inequality is an important aspect of systemic violence in schools.

Systemic violence in education may not be immediately noticeable but can be found woven into the educational fabric. We have attempted to identify and examine obvious and subtle forms of violence from a variety of educational perspectives: the organization of education, educational leadership, educational labeling, classroom interaction, childhood games, exclusive subject matter, and exclusive classroom practices.

This book is intended to illuminate some of the issues surrounding systemic violence. In part 1, we frame our work by providing an assessment of the overreaching structures and processes which are the schools themselves—the ways in which they are administered and the patterns and expectations of learning. In part 2, we examine the effects of these structures on children in the classroom. In part 3, we focus on a completely different aspect of systemic violence—its effect on teachers, especially women teachers who are attempting to operate within the existing structures. Finally, in part 4, we combine our thoughts and reflections to identify glimmers of hope and to recommend possible changes.

References

Cummins, J. (1989). *Empowering minority students*. San Diego, California: California Association of Bilingual Education.

Ellsworth, E. (1994). Why doesn't this feel empowering? Working through the repressive myths of critical pedagogy. In L. Stone (Ed.), *The education feminism reader*. New York: Routledge.

Fischer, L., Schimmel, D., and Kelly, C. (1991). *Teacher and the law*. New York: Longman.

Friedan, B. (1993). *The fountain of age*. New York: Simon & Schuster.

Freire, P. (1970). *Pedagogy of the oppressed*. Translated by M. B. Ramos. New York: Herder and Herder.

Government of Canada (1993). *Final report of the Canadian panel on violence against women*. Ottawa, ON: Minister of Supply and Service.

Ontario Ministry of Education. (1994). *Violence-free schools policy*. Toronto, Ontario: Queen's Printer for Ontario.

Kozol, J. (1991). *Savage inequalities: Children in America's schools*. New York: HarperCollins.

McPhedran, M. and Johnson, G. (1991). *The final report of the task force on sexual abuse of patients: An independent task force commissioned by the College of Physicians and Surgeons of Ontario*. Toronto, Ontario: College of Physicians and Surgeons.

Miller, A. (1990a). *For your own good*. New York: Noonday Press.

Miller, A. (1990b). *Banished knowledge*. New York: Doubleday.

Miller, A. (1990c). *The untouched key*. New York: Doubleday.

Ng, Roxana. (1993). Racism, sexism and nation building in Canada. In C. McCarthy and W. Crichlow (Eds.), *Race, identity, and representation in education* (p. 52). New York: Routledge.

Paquet, R. A. (1982). *Judicial rulings, state statutes and state administrative regulations dealing with the use of corporal punishment in public schools*. Palo Alto, California: R & E Research Associates.

Part I

Systemic Violence in
Administrative Practice

Chapter 1

Administrative Complicity
and Systemic Violence
in Education[1]

Ailsa M. Watkinson

Paulo Freire (1970) stated that any situation in which people are prevented from learning is one of violence (p. 73). The thrust of his seminal work was the exposition of the oppressor's role on the life and learning of the oppressed. The situation of oppression is, he states, "a dehumanized and dehumanizing totality affecting both the oppressors and those they oppress" (p. 32). To prevent others from learning is to violate their humanity.

Schooling bestows on educators oppressive power and authority while students are given almost none. Some may scoff at the notion of educators as oppressors, but there is no doubt that they have more power, control, and authority than their students. This was confirmed in a 1986 Canadian court decision (*R. v. J.M.G.*, 56 O.R. 2d, Ontario Court of Appeal) which ruled that students in school are "under detention of a kind throughout [their] school attendance," and are, therefore, "subject to the discipline of the school and required by the nature of [their] attendance to undergo any reasonable disciplinary or investigative procedure" (p. 712). The case sets an unfortunate precedent by limiting student rights under the *Canadian Charter of Rights and Freedoms*.

Educators set policies, practices, and cultivate conventions, which build a school culture. Unwittingly, the school culture may be a systemically violent culture that prevents a large number of students from learning. Such a culture of systemic violence is built, enforced, and reenforced by educators at a cost to those already

3

burdened by society's construct of their value and worth. While students are given equal access to an education, disparaging and discriminatory things happen on the way to graduation that result in unequal educational outcomes.[2] The inequities—the violence—are measured in stunted academic achievement, student dropout rates, and diminished student confidence.

At a time when educators are wringing their hands over "increased school violence" (Teacher Abuse Survey to Spark Debate, 1994), systemic violence is all the more insidious because it has, in part, been created by educational decision makers. Its creation is not usually intentional. Rather systemic violence results from traditional practices that may appear innocuous but which prevent or impede a student's learning.

The purpose of this chapter is to explore educational practices that are oppressive and discriminatory, thus preventing students from learning: systemic practices and procedures, built into the fabric of the system resulting in adverse burdens being placed on students. The first part of this chapter will define systemic violence as it will be used throughout the book. I will also examine how school practices and procedures dictated by the organization of schools, school leadership, and pedagogy impede the learning opportunities of students, contributing to a school culture imbued with violence. Educational systemic violence inflicts two types of harm. One results from the dehumanizing of students, which propels them to fail, drop out of school, and in some cases commit acts of aggression that culminate in their suspension or expulsion. The other harm is the production of discriminatory educational results emanating from a school culture that obfuscates the social, historical, legal, and economic differences among students. Finally, I will suggest institutional changes which will assist in eliminating educational systemic violence ensuring that no one is prevented from learning.

Systemic Violence

Systemic violence is any institutionalized practice or procedure that adversely impacts on disadvantaged individuals or groups by burdening them psychologically, mentally, culturally, spiritually, economically, or physically (Marshall and Vaillancourt, 1993). It is perpetrated by those with power, entitlement, and privilege against those who have less. Systemic violence results from conventional policies and practices which foster a climate of violence, and policies and practices that appear neutral but result in discriminatory effects. The Canadian Supreme Court's definition of discrimination is similar to that of systemic violence in that it takes into account the distribution of power and privilege and the imposition of the power and privilege on those who have historically been disadvantaged. The Court stated that legislation prohibiting discrimination "is designed to protect those groups who suffer social, political and legal disadvantage in our society" (*Andrews v. Law Society of British Columbia,* 1989, p. 325). Students fall into this category by virtue of their age,[3] the legal compulsion forcing them to attend school (*The Saskatchewan Education Act, s. 175*), the legal authority invested in educational decision makers, and the lack of authority given to students.[4]

Educational systemic violence results from the practices, procedures, and educational conventions that prevent students from learning, thus harming them. Freire (1970) wrote that dehumanization "is a distortion of being more fully human, sooner or later being less human leads the oppressed to struggle against those who made them so" (p. 28). The dehumanizing of students begins within a dehumanized education system.

Educational institutions are designed as oppressive bureaucracies devoid of interconnectedness and caring. Educational leadership is militaristic, macho, and looking for a fight. Traditional pedagogy, weighed down by organizational structure and leadership, is caught in the lamentable paradox of teaching democratic principles, the *sine qua non* of upholding human dignity, but practicing almost none.

The educational environment also blocks and impedes learning through conventional policies and practices that appear neutral on their face but result in discriminatory effects. Discrimination is systemic violence. It occurs when members of an identifiable group have been harmed because of their membership in that group. It too is an act of power perpetrated by those with entitlement and privilege against those with less. The harm caused by discrimination can be psychological, mental, cultural, spiritual, economic, or physical.

This type of violence arises from a dehumanized organization that is incapable of meeting the needs of students or from pedagogy's hidden curriculum reinforcing sexism, racism, and classism.

School violence is fostered by a systemically violent school culture which impedes learning by being unresponsive to students and the diversity among students. The real culprits in understanding school violence are school organization, school leadership, and school pedagogy: elements of school culture.

School Culture

The culture of violence built into the bricks and mortar of schools is acted out in the classrooms, the halls, and the playgrounds. Rarely is the violence motivated by ill will. In fact, to many, the policies and practices appear normal—quite ordinary—even harmless. But if these ordinary and everyday policies and practices burden or harm students psychologically, mentally, culturally, spiritually, economically, or physically, then they are violent.

School Organization

Contemporary school design is bureaucratic—based on the business model (Shakeshaft, 1989; Hodgkinson, 1991). This business model is far removed from the one-room centers of teaching which, by the late nineteenth century, were reorganized into "cost-efficient models of business" (Shakeshaft, 1989, p. 31) equipped with a C.E.O.—that is, a chief educational officer (a pathetic case of "Bay Street Wanabees")—and much talk about corporate structure, inputs and outputs, marketing of schools, and the bottom line.

The business model brought with it its bureaucratic structure characterized by "a hierarchy of personnel, tenure and careerism, role formalism, record keeping and paperwork, impartial and impersonal rules and regulations, professionalism and technical competence, committees and collective decision making, judicial process and unresponsiveness to changes in external or internal environment " (Hodgkinson, 1991, p. 54). The business model left behind a familial learning environment characterized by feelings of community and belonging, knowing others well, the personal touch, cooperation and caring. These differences between the business model and the familial learning environment are congruous with Carol Gilligan's ethic of justice (business) and ethic of care (familial) (Watkinson, 1992).

One of the many characteristics of a bureaucracy is "a horizontal division of graded authority or hierarchy, entailing supervision from above" (Ferguson, 1984, p. 7) and graded submission on the way down. And way down the educational hierarchy is the student (Miles and Fenn, 1989; West, 1988; Okin, 1989; Moss Kanter, 1977).

Ferguson (1984) believes bureaucracies epitomize the unequal distribution of power and dominance between men, women, and children. By this she is referring to the domination by men on the lives of women and children. Max Weber, the German architect of modern bureaucracies, viewed bureaucracies as a useful mode of social dominance attained by dehumanizing the workplace and eliminating from official business "love, hatred, and all personal, irrational, and emotional elements which escape calculation" (Moss Kanter, 1977, p. 18). The aim of bureaucracies is to arrange the workplace so as to secure continuity, stability, and consistency.

But learning within a dehumanized environment is unappealing to many students. A dehumanized learning environment contributes to their feelings of isolation and alienation. The anonymity and enforced isolation of large bureaucratic schools push students to drop out (Fine, 1991). A large percentage of dropouts are members of minorities, lesbians, gay men, and the poor (pp. 19–22). Thus, the very essence of a bureaucracy, its inherent domination and dehumanized environment, prevent these students from learning.

Violence among students has been blamed on the dehumanizing impersonal and detached conditions of school life manifested by bureaucracies (Ferguson, 1984, pp. 42–46). Isolation and alienation, under the veil of anonymity, make it easier to violently act out. Larger schools, heavier and oppressive bureaucracies, and higher student teacher ratios increase student isolation, alienation, and frustration (Fine, 1991). Aronowitz points to the various illicit activities that occur in school restrooms making them "the locus of resistance of students to total administration" (cited in Ferguson,

1984, p. 46). The administration Arnowitz speaks of is the type seen in most schools, one clearly defined by hierarchical structure and definite roles.

The rigidity and reliance on impersonal rules and regulations that mark bureaucracies are violent in other ways. They eclipse the circumstances of a particular student rendering her or him invisible. The result is that students who are different from the majority and require adjustments to the status quo, in order to learn, are often ignored. Decisions "grounded in considerations of sympathy, caring and an assessment of differentiated need are defined as not rational, not 'objective,' merely sentimental" (Young, 1987, p. 634). What counts in decision making is rationality, objectivity, impartiality.

The unwillingness or inability of educational decision makers to understand and empathize with the particular circumstances of students who are disadvantaged socially, politically, and legally has dire consequences on the ability of these students to learn. This point is illustrated in the lack of consideration given to mothers attending school. It has been and continues to be a struggle to convince educational decision makers to provide childcare so that mothers can learn. The struggle continues even though statistics show that 50 percent of single mothers drop out of school and 75 percent of married mothers drop out of school (Fine, 1991, p. 22). The consequence is almost certain poverty for the mothers and their children (p. 23). As long as girls get pregnant and schools turn a blind eye to their situation, the mothers will be victimized by the education system psychologically, mentally, and economically.[5] Even though the mothers are not denied entry into school they are bounced out by bureaucratic impartiality and apathy. As Ferguson points out, a bureaucracy "damages people in different ways at its different levels (1984, p. 88).

School Leadership

Theories on school leadership and the valued qualities of educational administration were developed from studying the military, corporations, and other institutions that had or have little, if anything, to do with children. Shakeshaft (1989, p. 148) devotes an entire chapter to the topic of "Androcentric Bias in Education

Administration and Research." In it she examines a number of theories and concepts that are commonly referred to in educational administration textbooks but that were developed by studying organizations virtually devoid of children .

Central to her deconstruction of leadership theory is its pervasive maleness. Writers have discussed the maleness of administration saying that the requisites of management are constructed from popular beliefs of the stereotypical male (Shakeshaft, 1989; Morgan, 1989; Brandt, 1992, p. 46). Thus the characteristics associated with leadership are those that describe maleness. According to Morgan, the qualities of leadership fit the western stereotypes of maleness. Qualities such as analytical, rational, and instrumental are valued while the qualities of nurturing and empathic support which are often associated with women, are undervalued. Leadership, he writes, "defines a man's world" (p. 211). Sergiovanni agrees. Management literature, he said, was traditionally written "by men for men, and its values—individualism, competition—define success in a masculine way" (cited in Brandt, 1992, p. 47).[6]

The military's connection to educational administration theory is especially troubling. Noble traces the military's interest in the unpredictable "human factor" during times of conflict and aggression to organizational theories and their application to the education of children (Noble, 1988, p. 241).[7] These military theories, adopted by educational leaders, were designed to gain an advantage over the enemy. *But who is the enemy?*

Even the language of educational administration is fraught with military words. Nothing illustrates this more than the popular use of the term "strategic planning."[8] According to the Oxford Dictionary (1989), the root word "strategy" means "to force (a person) into (a position) by strategy . . . the art of a commander-in-chief, the art of projecting and directing the larger military movements and operations of a campaign." The more conventional definition states: "In theoretical circumstances of competition or conflict, as in the theory of games, decision theory, business administration, etc., a plan for successful action based on the rationality and interdependence of the moves of the opposing participants." Strategic is defined as "pertaining to, or designating nuclear weapons intended to destroy an enemy's capacity to make war." *But who are we at war with? And who declared war?*

Mark, an urban teacher, thinks we are at war with students. His conversation concerning an issue of inequality at school was peppered with war metaphors such as "the longer you let the fuse smolder," "the more ammunition you bring into the issue," "I had to try to diffuse that and say, . . . let's leave all that other ammunition out of it," and "pretty soon you have a little army on one side and a little army on the other side" (Watkinson, 1993). If educational administrators, loaded with the artillery of military theory, machismo, and military language are preparing for war or have declared war, how can we blame students for fighting back? Perhaps it's self-defense.

Pedagogy

Pedagogy, as it is used here, means "the integration in practice of particular curriculum content and design, classroom strategies and techniques, and evaluation, purpose and method" (Rogers cited in McLaren, 1989, p. 161). All of these influence the learning atmosphere in the classrooms, the halls and the playground. Pedagogy, in turn, is influenced by school organization and leadership. As noted earlier, school organization and school leadership are typically rigid, authoritarian, and impersonal. In many ways, so is pedagogy. The result is more systemic violence.

Traditional pedagogy regards the student as the passive learner being schooled by an authority. The experiences and perceptions of students count for nothing. The same is true of democratic and egalitarian principles. The inherent dignity of each student is negotiated and perhaps granted if and when the student demonstrates her or his worth by evidence of acculturation: that is, deference to power and epistemic absolutes. For those who are not acculturated, "the school has its own arsenal of coercive weaponry—suspension, verbal abuse, corporal punishment, withholding of affection, denial of 'privileges' (recess, athletics, bathroom), and above all else the dreaded lower grade, or 'bad' reference" (Purpel, 1989, p. 47). As Connell points out, the violence inherent in this type of indoctrination is social control rather than liberation and empowerment (Connell, 1993).

While all students are the victims of this type of harm, there are other systemic practices that negatively affect females, gay and lesbian students, students who are racialized, have a disability, and who are economically disadvantaged. For example, the traditional authoritarian style of pedagogy has been identified as a systemic barrier to students who have been the victims of child sexual abuse (Brooks, 1992; Learning and Violence, 1992; Violence Prevention, 1992–1993). Studies show that 33 to 50 percent of children have been sexually abused (Bagley, 1991, pp. 103–104). To extrapolate, this means that in any classroom, one-third to one-half of the students have been sexually abused. Many others have been physically abused. The authoritarian hegemony is a continuation of other forms of abuse and increases the likelihood of these students failing or dropping out of school.

In addition, research has shown that traditional pedagogy favors boys' learning patterns more than girls' (Lather, 1991; Sadker and Sadker, 1994), teachers interact more with boys than girls and the interaction is more meaningful (Lather, 1991; Sadker and Sadker, 1994; Goodnow, 1994). The effect is that the learning environment stunts the intellectual growth of girls. Studies show that girls start school ahead of boys in reading and basic computation skills but by the time they graduate from high school boys have higher scores in both areas (White cited in McLaren, 1989, p. 184; Sadker and Sadker, 1994).

Girls also encounter a learning environment poisoned by sexual harassment (Stein, Marshall, and Tropp, 1993). The harassment of girls in schools by other students is often dismissed as flirting or a normal part of adolescence (pp. 3–4) but sexual harassment in schools is violent and a problem. As Zucker has noted:

> The academic environment existing at an educational institution is extremely important in determining the benefit that a student receives from attending that institution. A sexually abusive environment inhibits, if not prevents, a harassed student from developing her full intellectual potential and receiving the most from the academic program (A v. E., 1992, p. 326).

A recent study found that 92 percent of girls between the ages of twelve and sixteen years, who responded to a survey on sexual harassment, had been sexually harassed in school (LeBlanc, 1993, p. 134). Ninety-six percent were harassed by other students and 4 percent were harassed by teachers, administrators, or other school staff (Stein, Marshall, and Tropp, 1993, p. 6). The harassers in student to student cases were male 97 percent of the time. All but one of the adult harassers were male (p. 6).

The most common types of sexual harassment experienced by 89 percent of the young women were sexual comments, jokes, suggestive looks and gestures. Eighty-three percent reported being touched, pinched, or grabbed (Stein, Marshall, and Tropp, 1993, p. 6). The impact of this type of abuse takes its toll. Students spoke about their declining marks, their lack of self-confidence arising from the harassment[9] and an omnipresent fear of physical and sexual violence (Canadian Teacher's Federation, 1990, p. 14). The girls reported that only 8 percent of their schools had and enforced a policy on sexual harassment (Watkinson, 1995a).

The inability of administrators to deal effectively with sexual harassment in schools appears to be an example of what Gramsci calls "common sense" (Ng, 1993). "Common sense" is the taken-for-granted characteristic of the dominant group. Gramsci's "common sense" draws attention to normal and ordinary actions and practices whose banality renders them invisible (p. 52). Because the sexual harassment of students is considered so ordinary, so adolescent, so everyday, it is not seen as violence. The inability of educational decision makers to identify it as a form of violence and their inability to deal with it is due in large part to the fact that most educational decision makers are men and for many their "common sense" perceives sexual harassment differently than women. The differing perceptions of men and women regarding sexual harassment has led the courts to define the "reasonable woman" standard:

> We believe that in evaluating the severity and pervasiveness of sexual harassment, we should focus on the perspective of the victim. . . . A complete understanding of the victim's view requires, among other things, an analysis of the different perspectives of men and women. Conduct that many men consider unobjectionable may offend many women (*Ellison v. Brady*, 1991, p. 878).

The reasonable woman standard was expanded upon in *Robinson v. Jacksonville Shipyards, Inc.* (1991) and referred to in the Canadian case of *A v. E* (1992).

Gramsci's notion of "common sense" is also helpful in examining racism. Ng (1993) uses the unpunctuated phrase "gender race and class" to indicate that the concepts often function rhetorically to gain legitimacy rather than as a basis for analysis. The unpunctuated phrase also illustrates the interrelatedness of class to race to sex. Bannerji states: "It is entirely possible to be critical of racism at the level of ideology, politics and institutions . . . yet possess a great quantity of common sense racism" (1987, p. 10).

It is also entirely possible to teach tolerance yet possess a great quantity of common sense intolerance. The point is illustrated in the following conversation I had with a public school classroom teacher while conducting research into how educators deal with issues of inequality. "Lyle" begins each school day with the Lord's Prayer. I asked if all students participate.

Lyle: I've never had any problems . . . I have an East Indian girl in my class now. I've had several East Indian students in the past. They take part with the rest of the class.

Ailsa: They stand and recite the Lord's Prayer?

Lyle: Yes.

Ailsa: Is your student Christian or is she Hindu?

Lyle: I'd have to check her folder again but there's nothing there that makes me think that she's Hindu other than that her parents. . . . When I see her parents, they definitely look like they're practicing Hindus but really I couldn't say and it hasn't posed any problem.

Ailsa: Do you know why? I wonder why the parents wouldn't object.

Lyle: For the simple fact if they aren't Christian, if they are practicing Hindus, they're probably not going to say anything about saying the Lord's Prayer. I don't know if they've just come to the country recently and feel they don't want to make waves or they'd rather fit in. They may not understand how the school system works and what our rights and freedoms are in Canada or else they might just feel that they'd like their daughter to take part in whatever happens to be going on at school. There's a lot of different reasons.

Ailsa: But none of the parents have ever said anything to you?

Lyle: No, never.

Ailsa: Why do you think it is important to begin the school day with the Lord's Prayer?

Lyle: I believe there should be some sort of religious aspect to the school day. I'm Catholic myself but I don't press my religion on anyone else. But I think religion is a family value, it has a place that is disappearing and I don't think that kids realize today the importance of religion in their family life like kids ten or twelve years ago.

• • •

Ailsa: Do you not see a bit of a paradox in teaching about tolerance, teaching about different religions, teaching about prejudice and yet having an opening exercise that promotes Christian values?

Lyle: You could call it a paradox.

Ailsa: I just wonder what students think. What about a minority student who is in your class?

Lyle: I don't think at the grade five level you're going to get students thinking in those terms. . . . I've never even considered that but maybe they (members of minority groups) think that to be a good capitalist you have to have some religion and you have to have a lot of nationalistic attitude or whatever. . . . I guess it is a bit of a paradox but there's a lot of things that we teach in the education system that are a paradox because they just don't sit well together.

Lyle spoke the words and taught the lessons describing the virtues of equality, tolerance, and civic-mindedness but his "common sense" told him that state-led Christian practices offended none of those virtues. The educational decision makers in Lyle's school division allowed and indeed encouraged the use of Christian practices. The educational goals of the School Division were displayed on the walls of the school, one of which was to ". . . develop a knowledge and a respect for cultures, values, political and religious beliefs of others."

The violence caused religious minorities is emotional, spiritual, psychological, and physical. It may be as dramatic as it was for one young girl who was taught that she would "go to hell" if she was not Christian. During the time the student, a member of the Baha'i faith, was receiving Christian education instruction, she had recurring nightmares in which she was pursued by the devil and felt that she was burning in hell. A group of parents challenged the constitutional validity of providing religious instruction and also the provision allowing students to be exempt from the instruction which was, the parents argued, of little consequence since they feared their children would be further ostracized. The Ontario Court of Appeal agreed with the expert evidence of a psychology professor who said children will feel a pressure to conform to Christian beliefs that are sponsored and supported by the school. As a result, the students will experience stress and discomfort when confronted with the pressure to conform to a religious belief that they know is different from their own (*Canadian Civil Liberties Association v. Ontario,* 1990, p. 365).

Chris Tait, a young Manitoba student, objected to the reciting of the Lord's Prayer as part of the opening exercises at his school. His one person protest, with the support of his family, led to his ostracism, harassment and assault. Tait was to have been the valedictorian at his grade twelve graduation but was deprived of the honor after objecting publicly to the religious practice. On Chris Tait's graduation night he received seventy-five harassing and threatening calls in the twenty-four hours before the graduation ceremony. He attended the graduation party and saw himself burned in effigy. His night ended when he was locked in a granary all night. He would not reveal everything that happened to him, but said it was the scariest night of his entire life. His family members were also shunned and their property vandalized (Prayer Issue, 1989). Christian religious practices in schools do little to foster tolerance or respect for individual beliefs. History has shown that many wars have been fought over religious intolerance, and many individuals have been persecuted because of their beliefs.[10]

Common sense also obscures what is omitted from the curriculum. I recently asked a first-year university class of twenty-two students if they had read or been exposed to the history of Japanese-Canadian internment during the Second World War by the Canadian Government. I received a unanimous "no." I asked them if they knew about the Canadian Government's attempt to "Christianize and civilize" (Jaine, 1993) aboriginal people by forcing them to attend Residential Schools—a unanimous "no." I asked them if they knew that homosexuals, Gypsies and persons with disabilities were also the victims of Hitler's concentration camps—a unanimous "no." While my survey is small, it is compelling in that not one of the twenty-two students, in their twelve years of public schooling, had heard about the devastating inequalities and violence forced on groups and individuals who were different from the majority.

Finally, a household anecdote. My son was asked to do an assignment on St. John's, Newfoundland, for his grade three history class. One book he used mentioned that the Beotuk Indians lived in Newfoundland at the time Cabot arrived. Nothing more was said about them. No mention was made of the fact that there are no Beotuk Indians anymore and no mention was made of the fact that they were hunted and slaughtered by European settlers.

If students have not heard the history, how can we stop the violence and harm caused to those who have been historically disadvantaged and victimized? The old adage that "Those who do not remember the past are condemned to repeat it" is of little threat to those whose history has been privilege and power. It is devastating for those who have historically suffered psychological, mental, cultural, spiritual, and physical pain. The harm is compounded when we realize that the living and reliving of inequalities and violence has taken place because the majority do not know or do not care to know the past.

Addressing Systemic Violence

Throughout this book we will be placing emphasis on the ways in which schools and school systems can hope to eliminate systemic violence. Feminist scholars have called for changes in the organizing of institutions, one that transforms from a bureaucracy into a web of interconnectedness (Gilligan, 1982; Ferguson, 1984; Shakeshaft, 1989; Watkinson, 1993; Watkinson, 1995b). A similar point is made by Sergiovanni who proposes a change in the metaphor which describes educational institutions as organizations to one of communities (1994, p. 6). All press for an abandoning of organizational hierarchy and the creation of a humane community.

Research demonstrates that learning opportunities for students are enhanced within a humane environment (Matthews, 1991; Schultz et al., 1987; see also Monteath and Cooper and Ndunda in this book). Matthews reports that the intrinsic motivation in academic learning of girls and boys is increased in humanistic school settings as compared to students in more structured school environments. A humane or humanistic school setting is characterized by the "ethic of care" (Gilligan, 1982) which values connection and is concerned with problems of detachment, abandonment and indifference. The ethic of care is contrasted with the ethic of justice which values reciprocity and fairness. The ethic of justice is formal and abstract. A humanistic school setting is defined as a student-centered environment with small classes, student input in decision making and attention to individual needs. It is an atmosphere under which students and teachers get to know each other well—a community of teachers, administrators, and students working cooperatively, nurturing "fundamental humane and creative educational thinking, enabling them to bestow upon their pupils the happiness of school life and the joy of exchanging ideas with the teachers" (Amonashvili, 1989, p. 585). In addition, a nurturing, positive, and supportive environment promotes social connectedness, cooperative behavior, and creative and self-enhancing independence (Schultz, 1987, p. 32). Violence is rare in such environments; the interconnectedness and familiarity produce a world of caring where no one is left alone or hurt (Gilligan, 1982, p. 62).

If we change our metaphor of schools from organizations to communities, let us change our metaphor of chief education officer to community developer, midwife, educational care giver, or educational facilitator. But whatever the name, educators must be, above all, caring, compassionate, and empathic (Watkinson, 1994, p. 273). It is in dealing with matters of inequity and disadvantage that one's ability to "enter the skin" (Wilson, 1990, pp. 22–23) of the other, to empathize, and to sympathize, really counts. Educators who understand and care about the "differences" of others are moved to lessen their burden and improve their learning opportunities (Watkinson, 1994; Watkinson, 1995b).

Pedagogy must also be reshaped. First it must be reconstructed from the "standpoint of the least advantaged" (Connell, 1993; also Epp and Ndunda in this book). One Canadian court called upon educators to "stand in the shoes" of the least advantaged and reconsider "common sense" conventional practices (*Zylberberg et al v. Sudbury Board of Education,* 1988, p. 34). Participatory democracy is essential. The notion of participatory democracy requires the development of a curriculum that will include the experiences of women, Aboriginal people, members of other marginalized and racialized groups, and those who are poor. Participatory democracy means the valuing of student direction in decision making and curriculum planning. Finally education needs to ferret out all barriers to learning that hinder or obstruct any student's right to learn (see Whitty and Ho, Webb, and Hughson in this book). The consequence of doing otherwise is institutionalized violence and the diminished self-esteem of one too many students.

Educational decision makers have the legal mandate to provide educational equality and quality. (*The Saskatchewan Education Act,* 1978; *The Saskatchewan Human Rights Code;* 1979; *Canadian Charter of Rights and Freedoms,* 1982; *Convention on the Rights of the Child,* 1989). One of the duties and responsibilities of school administrators is to "maintain an environment in which learning takes place" (*New Jersey v. T.L.O.,* 1985, p. 743). The American decision was affirmed in a 1986 Ontario Court of Appeal case (*R. v. J.M.G.,* 1986, p. 708). To reconstruct educational institutions into environments in which every student can learn requires transformational change. Educators have the tools to do it.

Notes

1. An earlier version of this chapter was presented at the XXII Annual Conference of the Canadian Society for the Study of Education, Calgary, Alberta, Canada, June 1994.

2. Treating everyone the same does not meet the legal requirement of equality. Equality means equal outcomes and results. The Canadian Supreme Court has ruled that identical treatment may frequently produce serious inequality and that to realize true equality may mean treating others differently (Andrews v. Law Society of British Columbia [1989] 2 W.W.R. 289, p. 299).

3. The *Canadian Charter of Rights and Freedoms* prohibits discrimination on the basis of age.

4. See for example ss. 149,150,151, and 175 of *The Saskatchewan Education Act*. See also, R. v. J.M.G., 56 O.R. 2d (Ont. Ct. App.).

5. While slightly fewer women than men drop out of school, a woman's chances of finding paid work after she has dropped out of school is less than her male cohort (Fine, 1991, p. 259).

6. Sergiovanni discusses new ideas of leadership and admits to reading feminist scholarship and being taken aback by it. He states that "when I first began to read the feminist literature, I thought, 'who are these arrogant people?' But it turns out they were right." For further insight into Sergiovanni's changes in thought about leadership, see Thomas J. Sergiovanni, 'Why we should seek substitutes for leadership' (1992) *Educational Leadership 41* (49), 5.

7. Noble despairs that the processing of the mind, like the processing of a technical instrument, has lost "any consideration of the possibility that things could have been different—that our present 'cognitive' understanding of the mind, and of its role in society, is an historical invention whose hegemonic influence keeps us from considering alternative approaches to intellect, and . . . to the meaning of intellectual development within education" (Noble, 1988, p. 251). Thomas Greenfield (1986, p. 57) is extremely critical of the willingness of educational administration to accept the "scientific" organizational theories.

8. When conducting the research for this chapter I entered the term strategic planning into the library computer and no less than 118 citations appeared. The vast majority of them dealt with business planning.

9. Lack of self-confidence is a trait found too often in young women. The Canadian study, *We're Here Listen to Us* reported that "young women are less likely (than young men) to feel they have good qualities, to feel self-confident, and to feel good about themselves" (p. 25). The young women expressed feelings of powerlessness in relationships with boys. The feelings of powerlessness are tied to their feelings of low self-esteem which in turn "makes them all the more vulnerable to risks that particularly affect young women: sexual violence and unwanted pregnancy" (p. 41).

10. Rebell (1987) recounts how in a 1946 case in the United States, a young student objected to patriotic exercises on the basis of his religion. The Supreme Court of the United States ruled against him. When the

Supreme Court handed down its decision, the young boy was beaten and his father's store was boycotted (*Minersville School District v. Gobitis,*1946). The deeply religious Scottish philosopher, David Hume, condemned such Christian piety as serving no manner of purpose, saying, "we observe, on the contrary, that they [patriotic exercises] cross all these desirable ends; stupefying the understanding and harden the heart, obscure the fancy and sour the temper" (Hume, 1962, p. 219).

References

A.v.E. (1992). *Education & Law, 4.*

Amonashvili, S. (1989). Non-directive teaching and the humanization of the educational process. *Prospects*, 19.

Andrews v. Law Society of British Columbia (1989) 2 W.W.R. 289 at 299.

Aronowitz, S. (1973). False promises. In K. Ferguson, *The feminist case against bureaucracy* (p. 46). Philadelphia: Temple University Press.

Bagley, C. (1991). The prevalence and mental health sequels of child sexual abuse in a community sample of women aged 18 to 27. *Canadian Journal of Community Mental Health, 10* (1), 103–4.

Bannerji, H. (1987). Introducing racism: Notes towards an anti-racist feminism. *Resources for Feminist Research, 16*, 10.

Brandt, R. (1992). On rethinking leadership: A conversation with Tom Sergiovanni. *Educational Leadership, 49* (5).

Brookes, A. L. (1992). *Feminist pedagogy: An autobiographical approach*. Halifax: Fernwood.

Canadian Charter of Rights and Freedoms. Part I of Schedule B of the *Canada Act 1982*, R.S.C. 1985, App. 11, No 44.

Canadian Civil Liberties Association v. Ontario (Ministry of Education), (1990) 71 O.R. (2d.) 341 (Ont. C.A.).

Canadian Teacher's Federation. (1990). *A cappella: A report on the realities, concerns, expectations and barriers experienced by adolescent women in Canada* (p. 14). Ottawa: Canadian Teacher's Federation.

Connell, R.W. (1993). *Schools and Social Justice*. Toronto: Our Schools Our Selves.

Convention on the Rights of the Child, adopted by the General Assembly of the United Nations on November 20, 1989.

Ellison v. Brady, 924 F.2d 872 (9th Cir, 1991).

Ferguson, K. (1984). *The feminist case against bureaucracy*. Philadelphia: Temple University Press.

Final report of the Canadian panel on violence against women. (1993). Chairs: Pat Freeman Marshall and Marthe Asselin Vaillancourt, Ottawa: Ministry of Supply and Services.

Fine, M. (1991). *Framing dropouts: Notes on the politics of an urban public high school*. Albany, N.Y.: State University of New York Press.

Freire, P. (1970). *Pedagogy of the oppressed*. Translated by M. B. Ramos. New York: The Seabury Press.

Gilligan, C. (1982). *In a different voice: Psychological theory and women's development*. Cambridge: Harvard University Press.

Goodnow, C. (1994, April 18). Boys world: Girls education short changed by sexism. *Star Phoenix*, p. B15 [How Schools Shortchange Girls, American Association of University Women, 1992].

Greenfield, T. B. (1986). The decline and fall of science in educational administration. *Interchange, 17* (2), 57.

Hodgkinson, C. (1991). *Educational leadership: The moral art*. Albany, N.Y.: State University of New York Press.

Holmes, J. and Silverman, E. L. (1992). *We're here listen to us*. Ottawa: Canadian Advisory Council on the Status of Women.

Hume, D. (1962). *Inquiries: Concerning the human understanding and concerning the principles of morals*. 2nd ed. Oxford: Clarendon.

Jaine, L. (1993). *Residential schools: The stolen years*. Saskatoon: University of Saskatchewan Extension Division.

Lather, P. A. (1991). *Getting smart: Feminist research and pedagogy*. New York: Routledge.

Learning and violence: Women speak out (1992). Special issue of *Women's Education, 9* (4).

LeBlanc, A. N. (1993, May). Harassment at school: The truth is out. *Seventeen*, 134.

Matthews, D. B. (1991). The effect of school environment of intrinsic motivation of middle-school children. *Journal of Humanistic Education and Development, 30.*

McLaren, P. (1989). *Life in school: An introduction to critical pedagogy.* New York: Longman.

Miles, A. and Fenn, G. (Eds.) (1989). *Feminism from pressure to politics.* Montreal: Black Rose Books.

Minersville School District v. Gobitis 310 U.S. 586 (1946) Black Rose.

Morgan, G. (1989). *Images of organizations.* London: Sage.

Moss Kanter, R. (1977). *Men and women of the corporation.* New York: Basic Books.

New Jersey v. T.L.O (1985) 105 S.Ct. 733.

Ng, R. (1993). Racism, sexism, and nation building. In C. McCarthy and W. Crichlow (Eds.), *Race, identity, and representation in education* (p. 52). New York: Routledge.

Noble, D. D. (1988). Education, technology and the military. In L. E. Beyer and M. W. Apple (Eds.), *The curriculum: Problems, politics, and possibilities* (p. 241). Albany, N.Y.: State University of New York Press.

Okin, S. (1989). *Justice, gender, and the family.* New York: Basic Books.

Prayer issue settled, but Manitoba family is still shaken. (1989, March 25). *The Globe and Mail*, p. A1–A2.

Purpel, D. E. (1989). *The moral and spiritual crisis in education: A curriculum for justice and compassion.* Massachusetts: Bergin & Garvey.

R. v. J.M.G. (1986) 56 O.R. 2d (Ont. Ct. App.).

Rebell, A. (1987). Schools, values and the courts. *Yale Law and Policy Review, 7,* 275–342.

Robinson v. Jacksonville Shipyards, Inc. 760 F. Supp. 1486 (M.D. Fla. 1991).

Sadker, M. and Sadker, D. (1994). *Failing at fairness: How America's schools cheat girls.* New York: Scribner's.

Saskatchewan Education Act R.S.S. 1978, c.E-0.1.

Saskatchewan Human Rights Code. R.S.S. 1979, c. S-24.1.

Schultz, E. W. et al. (1987). School climate: Psychological health and well being in school. *Journal of School Health, 57.*

Sergiovanni, T. J. (1992). Why we should seek substitutes for leadership. *Educational Leadership, 49* (5), 41.

Sergiovanni, T. J. (1994). *Building community in schools.* San Francisco: Jossey Bass.

Sexual offences against children. (1984, August). In R. F. Badgley (Chair), *Report of the committee on sexual offences against children and youths, 1,* chap. 6. Ottawa: Canadian Government Publishing Centre.

Shakeshaft, C. (1989). *Women in educational administration.* Newbury Park: Sage.

Stein, N., Marshall, N. L., and Tropp, L. R. (1993). *Secrets in public: Sexual harassment in our schools.* Wellesley, Massachusetts: Center for Research on Women, Wellesley College, NOW Legal Defense and Education Fund.

Teacher abuse survey to spark debate. (1994, May 13) *Saskatchewan Bulletin, 1.* Saskatoon, Sask.: Saskatchewan Teachers' Federation.

The Oxford English Dictionary (1989). 2nd ed., vol. 16. Oxford: Clarendon.

The Saskatchewan Education Act (1978). Regina: Saskatchewan Queen's Printer.

Violence prevention (1992–1993). Special Issue of *Women's Education, 10* (1).

Watkinson, A. M. (1992). *Caring and justice in education: A charter challenge.* (Doctoral Dissertation, University of Saskatchewan, 1992). [unpublished].

Watkinson, A. M. (1993, June). *Inequality and or hormones.* Paper presented at the meeting of the Canadian Association for the Study of Educational Administration, Ottawa, ON.

Watkinson, A. M. (1994). Equality, empathy and the administration of education. *Education and Law Journal, 5* (3) 273–304.

Watkinson, A. M. (1995a). Hostile lessons: Sexual harassment in schools. *The Canadian Administrator 34* (1), 1–12.

Watkinson, A. M. (1995). Valuing women educators. In S. M. Natale and B. M. Rothschild (Eds.), *Values, work, education: The meanings of work* (pp. 107–130). Atlanta: Rodopi.

West, R. (1988). Jurisprudence and gender. *University of Chicago Law Review, 55* (1), 64–65.

White, D. (1983, March). After the divided curriculum. *The Victorian Teacher, 7.*

Wilson, B. (1990, February 8). *Will women judges really make a difference?* The Fourth Annual Barbara Betcherman Memorial Lecture, North York, ON, Osgoode Hall Law School, York University.

Young, I. M. (1987). Impartiality and the civic public. In S. Benhabib and D. Cornell (Eds.), *Feminism as critique: On the politics of gender* (p. 634). Minneapolis: University of Minnesota Press.

Zylberberg et al. v. Sudbury Board of Education, (1988) 29 O.A.C. 23 (On. C.A.).

Chapter 2

Authority, Pedagogy, and Violence

Juanita Ross Epp

Buried in the pervasively traditional mind-set of our school systems is an assumption that authority is a suitable basis for pedagogy. Authority is "power over" and authority in school is conferred on teachers and principals twice—first through their roles and secondly through their knowledge. Authority gives teachers, and especially principals, explicit permission to use violence as a means of correction. In Canada, this is spelled out in section 43 of the *Criminal Code*. Of course, the striking of children must be reserved for "correction" and must not be "excessive." It is left to the judgment of the teacher or principal to decide how much correction is necessary (see Tite in the next chapter).

Correction is usually considered necessary when students defy authority and thus compromise their "learning." In many schools, obedience is closely associated with learning, and disobedient children are assumed not to be learning. This linking of the expectations associated with authority and the application of authority to "sound" pedagogy and the inherent violence of this process, has strongly influenced what happens in our schools.

The link between pedagogy and authority was established in chapter 1. In this chapter it will be argued that these links are not in our students' best interests and that violence is a subtext of traditional authoritarian structures and traditional pedagogical methods. Part of the issue is hidden in the complexities of the genderization of school authority structures. This theme is taken up again in part 3 of this book.

The Violence of Authoritarian Structures

The use of authority in schools often serves to alienate students and encourage adversarial relationships between teachers and students (see chapter 1). Punishment and obedience training in schools have developed through an aberration of good intentions. Children have long been trained in obedience and acceptance of authority as one of the basics of education, but learning can be subverted by the need to control students and preserve a safe learning environment. Now that we are beginning to understand and identify the links between domination and societal violence, our schools must take responsibility for their role in maintaining the status quo by force.

Alice Miller (1990a, 1990b, 1990c) has advanced a passionate philosophical argument against authoritarian processes in child rearing. She argues that as long as we inflict punishment on children "for their own good" (1990b) we destroy their sense of self and their innate belief in their own worth. The worst part of this process is that the punishment itself destroys the children's mechanisms for understanding that such punishment is wrong. The children afraid to doubt or question their parents (or teachers) are disallowed their anger and internalize the abuse as being (a) something that they deserve and (b) something that loving parents (or teachers) must do to children. Thus, when they themselves attain positions of authority, they have a wellspring of anger and righteousness that fuels their treatment of subordinates, and so the cycle is perpetuated. They grow up believing that punishment is not only right but necessary.

Amid the continuing legal and moral battles over corporal punishment, Miller suggests that adults who hit children do it in response to their own unresolved anger. The children, on the other hand, forbidden to show aggression toward their parents and teachers, internalize the anger which will eventually be recycled in their treatment of others. This perception of the origins of violence has been taken a step further by Stettbacher (1991) who feels that criminal behavior is the delayed result of bottled up childhood aggression:

> Biographies of criminals . . . give us plenty of information on the origin of criminal behavior . . . If parents fail to respect and satisfy

their children's needs, their sons and daughters will later transfer their claim to other people and institutions. Using violence or manipulation they will attempt to force the world at large to respect and satisfy their, by now perverted, needs (pp. 107–108).

School authorities who condone violence as a means for controlling children are confirming their students' perceptions that "might is right," and this will, in turn, precipitate various acts of rebellion (Gordon, 1974). Negative experiences with power relationships may encourage young people, especially boys, to seek to reestablish their own position of dominance through violence. Authoritarian disciplinary tactics may prevent disruptions for the time being, but they are likely to result in future problems for both the children and for others with whom they will have power-based relations.

Gordon (1974) has long advocated the use of democracy and respect when dealing with school children. In his view, "teacher power," or authoritarian methods of dealing with students, is not only injurious to children, but also to the teachers using it. Children controlled in this manner become people who rely on authoritarian power and expect to be controlled by it. Our principals' offices are full of these children, waiting for one more confrontation in a series of battles that they will never win:

> Students who use power are just as liable to be corrupted. They are likely to become tyrants, and, in their tyranny, disrespectors of the feelings, needs, and property of others . . . It is terribly difficult to feel kindly toward these youngsters (Gordon, 1974, p. 212).

Children who are used to obeying only because they fear punishment are difficult to direct through other means, yet many teachers who have chosen not to use authoritative methods have been able to "control" their classrooms. Women teachers in particular have learned to use inclusive problem-solving approaches in order to address behavior. Be it by respect, humor, understanding, or inventiveness, they have been able to win over unruly students. Unfortunately, these people have always been in a minority and are unlikely to attain positions of authority. It is a modern irony that although many school boards have forbidden the use of corporal punishment, they have persisted in hiring principals who could administer such punishment should it become necessary.

Miller (1990c) would say that it is not too late to start the healing process. However, we would have to change our existing educational patterns. Schools and other social institutions could be instrumental in helping children come to terms with unresolved feelings, thus enabling them to become more effective adults:

> When the anger of early childhood and the ensuing grief have been experienced, affirmative feelings, which are not based on denial or feelings of duty or guilt, can emerge of their own accord, assuming the right preconditions are present (Miller, 1990c, p. 23).

It is in the provision of the "right preconditions" that administrators can make their most important contributions. Administrators, both male and female, could work toward changing attitudes about children and ensuring that schools build strong, courageous, supportive people in place of the controllers and the controlled. The day-to-day integration of intellectual and affective development would require a completely different view of pedagogy.

Pedagogy and Authority

> It is a mistake to suppose that education alone can solve this world's problems. Yet if there is to be hope of the continuation of life on earth, let alone of a good life for all, as educators we must strive to do more than join mind and body, head and hand, thought and action (Martin, 1994, p. 403).

How can schools combat the fragmentation of alienated feelings and unresolved abuses of power and hope to build honest equitable relationships between adults and children? Cooperative learning, holistic language, variety in teaching strategies, affective connections in skill building—all philosophically connected to teacher and student empowerment—are already fighting for a place on the curriculum. Basic to this changing view of children and child-rearing practices is a revised view of education, which has sometimes been dubbed "feminist pedagogy," although it will be referred to here as inclusive pedagogy. What sets "inclusive" pedagogy apart from others is (a) a belief in the importance of the affective; (b) a conviction that true education must include recognition and analysis of dominance and submission in social structures; and (c) the recognition of the personal affects of child abuse.

Inclusive pedagogy places emphasis on the importance of emotions, feelings, and personal responses. The lack of attention to the "affective" needs of our children teaches them to mask their feelings and disown their emotions:

> I had not been taught to critique the world as it appeared to me. Instead, years of uncritical, rote learning had taught me how not to know (Brookes, 1992, p. 2).

Schools would need to meet students' affective needs in order to allow access to cognitive domains. Inclusive pedagogy insists that education should facilitate the personalized interpretation of life experiences to enable students to recognize and deal with abuse, injustice and inequality. Although Brookes (1992) intended this approach to help females to come to grips with male domination, it could also be applied to young men dealing with the lack of opportunity to express emotion in their lives and those who need to resolve childhood traumas associated with power and control. Both boys and girls benefit from learning how to express and understand inequities in power structures.

Young men and women are equally at risk of being adversely affected by the structural social inequities imbedded in our culture. The difference is that young women tend to express their hidden rage by doing damage to themselves while young men tend to take it out by doing damage to others (see Jadwin in this book). As Steinem (1992) has pointed out: "Since men are more likely to respond to past abuse by abusing others, our prisons are full of those who continued to do to others what was done to them" (p. 79). The school system could provide the vital link in addressing these destructive tendencies. Brookes's theories would apply equally well to the education of boys and girls. Try this passage without the words in italics:

> Relations of power can work to produce the well-kept secret of *male* violence *against women*. It is a terrible violence. And it is reproduced through schooling practices . . . which work only too well to reinforce feelings of fear, inadequacy and contempt—teaching us that it is not nice, not scholarly and certainly not scientific to speak of the personal in an academic context (Brookes, 1992, p. 10, italics added).

The "autobiographical approach" advocated by Brookes (1992) is just one of many techniques used in inclusive pedagogy. It embraces practices which emphasize the shift from the importance of content to the importance of process. It would include activities in which students learned to value their own feelings—and those of others—and processes in which students were invited to problem solve and create rather than memorize and manipulate. Inclusive pedagogy encourages notions of "voice" and active learning and a linking of the affective with the cognitive. Pedagogical practices might include peer editing, life writing, letter writing, deconstruction exercises, role playing, dramatic reenactments, and class logs. The techniques are not as important as the provision of a risk-free environment in which half-formulated thoughts can be aired, accepted, and honed into meaning without fear of derision.

Inclusive teaching practices are intended to lead to a repositioning of society's values. Without that repositioning, teachers will continue to teach in the ways in which they have been taught and will carry on the "oppression" (Freire, 1970). The adoption of such a pedagogy would require a rethinking of the "common sense" beliefs about education outlined in chapter 1. This would require a "problematic" stance in which students and teachers question accepted "truths" in light of the societal assumptions which have allowed them to survive.

This rethinking is already going on. Martin (1994), for example, suggested that educators might rethink the need for subjects and disciplines. Rather than argue about which subjects should be taught, she suggested an examination of the whole concept of "subjects" (p. 188). Noddings (1992) suggested a new curriculum in which "caring" was applied to all elements of learning.

These ideas demand a rethinking of existing theories that have come to be held as sacred. For example, Maslow's hierarchy of needs, which was based on a study of "42 great men" (two of whom were women), might be reexamined and schools could be encouraged to spend more time on "belonging" and less on individual accomplishments. The standard learning curve, still taught in many teacher education institutions, remains the foundation for standardized testing. The mathematical probability that a small percent of our students will be "brilliant" while an equal number will be lacking in intellectual capacity is based more on mathematical speculation than reality. What then is the value of standardized tests?

> Through surveillance, observation, and classification [we] normalize children but do not seem to acknowledge or even understand the point that the developing child is an "object" produced by those very same practices (Ball, 1990, p. 12).

A revised attitude toward learning would be necessary for change. Perry (1970) recognized knowledge to be a life skill applied to personal and professional problem solving with different kinds of knowledge for different contexts. There are no absolute truths or complete answers. The learner's task is to identify the issues and seek the solutions according to the situation.

This is reminiscent of Freire's "liberating pedagogy" in which the teacher and the student are expected to learn simultaneously—through dialogue, reflection, and action along with humility, faith, hope, and communion. For Freire, content is secondary to dialogue, with students and teachers "together seeking reality." (1970, p. 33) Freire's (1970) work links with Alice Miller's (1990b) concern that many children grow up not realizing that the abuse they suffered as children was neither necessary nor normal. Freire identified the problem as lack of recognition. By accepting the oppression as necessary and even helpful, we have made ourselves incapable of the critical evaluation process which would be necessary to set us free:

> How can the oppressed, as divided, inauthentic beings, participate in developing the pedagogy of their liberation? Only as they discover themselves to be hosts of the oppressor can they contribute to the midwifery of their liberating pedagogy (Freire, 1970, p. 33).

"Inclusive pedagogy" is being undertaken by individuals working in isolated contexts to make their classrooms more inclusive. These isolated attempts are often smothered by outside structures unable to accommodate the changed philosophy. For example, one teacher reported extremely high grades for all of her students. These students had failed the regular grade nine mathematics program. They committed themselves to group processes with the goal of achieving mastery learning. The resulting A pluses on the report cards upset the regular mathematics teacher, the other students, the parents, and the administration. The teacher was accused of various unprofessional practices and the students were accused of cheating. The administrator's reaction was an important factor in the individual teacher's decision to challenge the status quo. A changed role for administrators would be necessary to create an environment in which alternative pedagogy could flourish.

Authority, Pedagogy, and Women Administrators

Although not alone in changing attitudes and processes, women are often credited with implementing change. If women were placed in positions of power in the school system, it would affect pedagogy as well as the genderization of schooling. When men run the schools and women work in them, boys are told that they will be bosses and girls are told that they will be subordinates even before they have opened a textbook. Standard ways of administering schools reinforce the dominance and subordination structure which remains the basis of our social ordering.

There are those who would argue that the position of school administrator from its very inception was based on power differentials. Blackmore (1989), for example, suggested that the separation of the roles of administrator and teacher early in the 1900s was not just an attempt to emulate the scientific management theories of the day but was an excuse to give male teachers an added measure of authority as well as someone to be in authority over. Structural reinforcement of male authority perpetuated the culturally imbedded assumptions of male supremacy:

The gendered and hierarchical distinction between administration and teaching as categories of work based on expertise, rather than as inextricably dependent and within the same field of practice . . . reinforce(s) existing power relations and the ways in which femininity and masculinity are socially constructed and reproduced in schools (Blackmore, 1989, p. 109).

Men came "naturally" to the role of administrator; women were not even considered for administrative posts, although they were valued as teachers because they were cheap labor. To quote the Quincy Board of Education, during the 1870s:

One man could be placed in charge of an entire graded school of 500 students. Under his direction could be placed a number of female assistants. Females are not only adapted, but carefully trained, to fill such positions as well as or better than men, excepting the master's place, which sometimes requires a man's force; and the competition is so great, that their services command less than half the wages of male teachers (cited in Shakeshaft, 1989, p. 31).

Such blatantly sexist staffing of a publicly funded school system could only exist in a society so completely grounded in gender discrimination as to be totally accepting of it. European-based forms of government evolved from a structure which required obligations of rank in both governance and religion (Jones, 1993). Family structures are founded on the same principles: if men "rule" their "castles," women and children must be subservient. The ideals of universal suffrage, independence, and free speech have forced a radical change in our governing structures, but this freedom from the chain of command has not necessarily included our offices, our schools, our churches, or our homes. Our society aspires to democratic principles and individual rights, but demands compliance from workers (teachers), women and children. Although society at large claims to have progressed beyond obedience and control in governance, the domination and subordination rituals remain in all other areas. As Brookes (1992) suggests:

Until women can reclaim and know authority, men will continue to abuse and victimize us and we will continue to please and follow men. Our society is organized to make it so (p. 31).

Some jurisdictions are working toward an alternative to the entrenchment of the present social order by ensuring that women hold at least half of the administrative positions. This would do more than serve as modeling for a more egalitarian future, it would also allow women an opportunity to redefine the school culture. There is growing evidence that when women administer they are likely to do it differently than men (Blackmore, 1989; Shakeshaft, 1989). Female administrators may be changing the way authority is practiced in schools. If children are learning their dominance and submission roles through us, by changing the daily transactions in the schools we can remove support from existing structures and discourage the reenactment of our history in their future.

Conclusion

It has been argued that women should occupy school administrative positions in equal numbers with men because their presence would change societal expectations for the dominant-subservient positions of men and women, and encourage a changed view of authority. This would foster a change in attitude toward discipline, punishment, and the treatment of young people, especially those children who may be responding in negative ways to abuses of authority in their own lives.

A changed view of authority would require a rethinking of education and an application of inclusive pedagogy. This would allow students to connect with their personal emotions, understand the dynamics of power and abuses of power, develop personal goals and challenges, and be encouraged in their abilities to relate to other people and use group processes in problem solving.

The argument presented here places administrators with the ability to modify the interpretation of authority at the center of a revised notion of education and society. Miller's (1990b) view of traditional child rearing practices as "institutionalized abuse" connects violence to the issues of domination and authority. Brookes (1992) takes institutionalized dominance into her arguments in support of "feminist pedagogy." Both of these views find their home in postmodern theoretical examinations of existing societal structures and individualized responses to them. Making the connection between authority and violence helps us understand "incorrigible" students among us; changing our fixation on control and replacing it with empathy allows us to meet the needs of all students.

The role of women in this transformation is multifold. First, the presence of women in positions of added responsibility would challenge the expectation that men will lead and women will follow and would provide models of mutuality and respect. Administrators would then be free to challenge traditional authoritarian values embedded in the school system and work toward replacing them with inclusive pedagogy based on personal worth, dignity, and respect (see part 3 of this book). These revised pedagogies would furnish students with the tools necessary to get in touch with their own emotions and to develop critical thinking skills, social and interpersonal skills, and problem-solving abilities. Then the real education process could begin—for all of us.

In rebellion alone, woman is at ease, stamping out both prejudices and sufferings; . . . women will sooner or later rise in rebellion (Louise Mitchell, 1890).

Note

1. A previous version of this paper was included in the proceedings of the American Association of University Women Conference held in Orlando, Florida, June 1995.

References

Ball, S. (ed.) (1990). *Foucault and education* London: Routledge.

Blackmore, J. (1989). Educational leadership: A feminist critique and reconstruction. In J. Smyth (Ed.), *Critical perspectives on educational leadership*. London: Falmer.

Brookes, A. (1992). *Feminist pedagogy: An autobiographical approach*. Halifax, N.S.: Fernwood.

Freire, P. (1970). *Pedagogy of the oppressed*. Translated by M. B. Ramos. New York: Herder & Herder.

Gordon, T. (1974). *T.E.T. Teacher effectiveness training*. New York: David McKay.

Jones, K. (1993). *Compassionate authority: Democracy and the representation of women*. New York: Routledge.

Martin, J. R. (1994). *Changing the educational landscape*. New York: Routledge.

Maslow, A. H. (1970). *Motivation and personality*. New York: Harper and Row.

Miller, A. (1990a). *Banished knowledge*. New York: Doubleday.

Miller, A. (1990b). *For your own good*. New York: The Noonday Press.

Miller, A. (1990c). *The untouched key*. New York: Doubleday.

Noddings, N. (1992). *The challenge to care in schools*. New York: Teachers College.

Perry, W. Jr. (1970). *Forms of intellectual and ethical development in the college years: A scheme*. New York: Holt, Rinehart & Winston.

Shakeshaft, C. (1989). *Women in educational administration*. Newbury Park: Sage.

Steinem, G. (1992). *Revolution from within*. Boston: Little, Brown & Co.

Stettbacher, J. K. (1991). *Making sense of suffering*. New York, Dutton.

Chapter 3

Who Knows? Who Cares?
Schools and Coordinated Action
on Child Abuse[1]

_____

Rosonna Tite

Since the mid-1970s, researchers and governments have been trying to persuade teachers to deal with the problem of child abuse and there has been plenty of recent policy activity on this issue (McEvoy, 1990; McIntyre, 1990). Most provincial and state legislation and school district directives are aimed at developing what many school boards now take pride in calling "coordinated action" (Mahony, 1989). The form it takes varies somewhat from place to place, but coordinated action on child abuse generally means that when teachers confront a suspicious incident or any symptoms that seem suggestive of abuse, they are required to report their suspicions, often through the principal or a designated senior teacher, to a child welfare agency. The agency investigates the case and coordinates assistance from a variety of sources, including the police, medical personnel, mental health professionals, and so on.

As feminists, we may well breathe a sigh of relief. Estimates indicate that as many as 50 to 60 percent of child abuse victims are of school age; the school is the primary institution concerned with children; and teachers may be the only trusted adults in a position to help (Abrahams, Casey and Daro, 1992; Beck, Ogloff and Corbishley, 1994; Maher, 1987). In addition, coordinated action seems to be putting forward the message that child abuse will no longer be tolerated—the teacher might find out.

But, in the midst of teachers' increased responsiveness, as feminists we remain unsettled about the role of the school and we

37

continue to focus attention on the ways that schools condone and perpetuate family violence. This is because we believe that abuse has its roots in biased values about gender roles and power relationships, attitudes developed in the early socialization experiences in the home and the school, and we are concerned about the school's continued involvement in punitive and authoritarian practices (Cole, 1985). If we seem ambivalent about the teachers' new surveillance role, it is because we continue to find ample evidence that schools create a culture of systemic violence, and we fear that "coordinated action" represents little more than an attempt to mask this inherent bias, while continuing the perpetuation of male dominance over women and children (Mahony, 1989; Tite, 1994a).

The necessity of a careful examination of coordinated action has become increasingly clear to me since I reported my first child abuse case in 1980. I was reminded of it again when I was teaching an introductory course on the contemporary classroom. The course included a school observation component, and we were discussing incidents the students had witnessed in the schools the day before. One young man told us that he was walking down the corridor with his host teacher at the noon hour as students were standing about, checking their lockers and chatting with friends on their way to the cafeteria. He was very surprised, he said, when his host teacher told him urgently to "put his hands in his pockets." He was compliant, of course, but puzzled. When he questioned the teacher later, he was told that "if you walk down the hall and accidentally touch a student with your hands, you could get charged with child abuse." Remarkably, few of my students seemed very surprised at the incident. There appeared to be a general consensus that "child abuse is a major issue in the schools" and that "male teachers are particularly vulnerable to false allegations."

If we dismissed the class response and simply discussed the evidence that adult males are more likely to be perpetrators of abuse than the victims of vicious lies, we would miss the main issue of this incident. Teachers' views about child abuse arise out of a social climate and institutional context which deserves more careful scrutiny. It is not just individual teachers who make decisions about reporting child abuse. The choices teachers make are embedded in a systemic predisposition toward supporting the myth of the safe and nurturant nuclear family, within longstanding ideas about the proper separation of the home and school. They are grounded in notions about the rights of parents to raise their children as they wish, and in the context of profound historical uncertainties about the use of punishment and authoritarian teaching practices.

Coordinated action is conducted in a particular context of procedural constraint and opportunity. The surveillance action itself, which requires teachers to turn abused children over to outside agencies, reinforces the old idea that child abuse is a marginal social or medical issue, and not a widespread problem deserving the full attention of educators. The way male and female teachers are positioned in the system, with women predominantly teaching in the primary and elementary grades, and men in the secondary school and in administrative roles, may profoundly influence not only educational ideas about child abuse, but also the types of abuse and kind of victims that are identified.

The Study

The findings described here are part of a larger three-part study of coordinated action. The project is aimed at documenting teachers' suspicions and reporting of child abuse cases and exploring the compatibility (or incompatibility) of mandatory reporting requirements with the "ordinary" work of the school. The first stage of the research involved a survey of a stratified random sample of teachers in kindergarten through grade twelve. For the second stage, I interviewed all willing survey respondents (33) who stated that they had made official reports of abuse. Here I will focus on the survey responses of 336 teachers (approximately 60 percent female, 40 percent male). The teachers were first asked to examine vignettes and decide whether or not they would report the abuse described in them. Then they were asked to provide information about any real cases they may have encountered.

Defining Abuse: The Vignettes

When teachers confront a suspicious situation, they enter into a complicated decision-making process which begins with their own judgment that a serious act of violence has taken place. Not all teachers who decide to apply the child abuse label will proceed to make a report, but it seems clear that if a report is going to be made, the process begins with thoughts about what child abuse actually is (Herzberger, 1988; Maney, 1988).

How teachers settle on their own definitions of abuse is not easily determined. Nor is there sufficient evidence to suggest an obvious relationship between the available legal definitions and intervention. An abused or neglected child is legally defined as one "whose physical or mental health or welfare is harmed or threatened with harm by the acts or omissions of his/her parent or other persons responsible for his/her welfare" (Government of Newfoundland and Labrador, 1993, p. 6). The definition includes four specific categories: sexual exploitation, physical harm, emotional abuse, and neglect, which includes physical and emotional neglect.

Although the official definition of abuse seems straightforward, the results of this survey suggest that there is a multidimensional and complex interplay between definitions, teachers' past experiences with cases, and school and agency response. In addition, the gender of the teacher and, depending on the type of abuse, the gender of the victim and perpetrator, appear also to be a critical influence.

In order to explore teachers' working definitions, I included ten short hypothetical vignettes in the questionnaire that were designed to determine how teachers apply the abuse label. Each vignette describes a situation a teacher might confront, i.e., a disclosure, an observation of a particular incident, a set of observations accumulated over a period of time, or a teachers' intuitive feelings. These included two each for physical, sexual, emotional abuse, and neglect, as well as two others dealing with children's learning needs. There is also an additional interesting twist. In the two vignettes for sexual abuse, I altered the gender of the victim; and in the vignettes describing neglect, I changed the gender of the perpetrator. The two versions of the questionnaire were randomly distributed throughout the sample to explore the extent to which male and female teachers would agree or disagree on the use of the "abuse" label, and to gain a broader understanding of the role of gender in this labeling practice.

The findings are summarized in Tables 1 and 2. Table 1 demonstrates that teachers go far beyond narrow legal definitions when they think "theoretically" about child abuse, preferring to include a range of behaviors often considered mild or marginal by child welfare agencies. In fact, while there is a general pattern to the data suggesting that men are less likely than women to apply the abuse label overall, the only vignette that stands out as not representing a case of child abuse is the one which describes spanking. This is a finding which perhaps speaks rather eloquently to the issue of teachers' uncertainties about discipline and punishment.

Besides confirming other studies which show that agency personnel are frequently impatient with teachers for their habit of referring nonurgent cases (Zellman, 1990), the teachers' vignette responses raised serious questions about how abuse gets officially defined and acted upon, and why teachers' obvious concerns for children's emotional and intellectual needs are overlooked. This is a key issue since much of the policy activity surrounding coordinated action is focused on developing legal definitions that are sufficiently clear to permit easy detection.

Although these results are, by and large, consistent with the results of my earlier survey (Tite, 1993), a gender analysis provides an interesting departure. First, as Table 1 indicates, men teachers seem less inclined than women to designate the sexual abuse vignettes as abusive. More than 75 percent of the women and just over two-thirds of the men applied the abuse label to the vignette describing a teacher's suspicion of incest. More than half of the women designated a child's exposure to pornography as abusive while just over one-third of the men did so. These differences are statistically significant.

A second significant result is put forward in Table 2. These figures describe the use of the abusive label for the four vignettes altered by the gender of victim and perpetrator. While the gender of the victim is not significant for incest (perhaps because the sexual abuse of boys was given widespread recent publicity in Newfoundland following the events at Mount Cashel), it is interesting that

Table 1
Use of the Child Abuse Label (N=327)

Vignettes	Male (n=124) n	Male (n=124) %	Female (n=203) n	Female (n=203) %
Physical				
Teacher observes bruise on child's face	76	65.0	147	74.2
Child discloses spanking for misbehavior	30	25.4	56	28.3
Sexual				
Teacher suspects incest (intuitive)	77	66.4	151	76.6*
Child shows teacher parents' pornography	48	41.0	105	53.0
Emotional				
Parent refuses psychological treatment for self-destructive child	94	79.7	155	78.7
Teacher suspects withdrawn behavior due to parents' violent fighting	54	45.8	105	53.0
Neglect				
Teacher observes that child is unclean	74	62.7	123	62.4
Teacher suspects inadequate after-school supervision (intuitive)	62	52.5	105	53.0
Other				
Teacher suspects learning disability but parents refuse psych-ed testing	66	55.9	115	58.1
Teacher recommends vision and hearing test but parents refuse	86	72.9	134	67.7

*Chi-Square 8.34 (df=3) $p < .05$

not only are women teachers more likely than men to use the abuse label for exposure to pornography overall, but they also seem slightly more inclined to designate exposure to pornography as abusive when the victim is female rather than male. This suggests that it is women teachers who are likely to be on the alert for sexual abuse symptoms, especially when they discover that a girl has been given access to pornographic material. While the vignettes do not establish a connection between pornography and sexual abuse, these results do raise questions about school attitudes toward pornography and leave us to wonder about the role of this material in the socialization of children, especially young boys.

Table 2
Use of the Child Abuse Label by Gender of Victim,
Perpetrator and Teacher-Selected Vignettes

	Version 1 victim/perpetrator		Version 2 victim/perpetrator	
	n	%	n	%
Incest	female/male		male/male	
Female Teacher	75	78.9	76	74.5
Male Teacher	40	69.0	37	63.8
Exposure to Pornography	male/male		female/male	
Female Teacher	44	46.3	61	59.2
Male Teacher	23	39.7	25	42.4
Neglect Cleanliness	male/female		male/male	
Female Teacher	58	61.7	65	63.1
Male Teacher	44	74.6	30	50.8*
Neglect Supervision	female/female		female/male	
Female Teacher	51	53.7	54	52.4
Male Teacher	33	55.9	29	49.2

*Chi-Square 7.11 (df=2) p < .05. Respondents were sent either Version 1 or Version 2 of the vignettes randomly as follows: Version 1: Males = 59 Females = 94. Version 2: Males = 59 Females = 103.

A third issue has to do with the vignettes describing neglect. The first vignette describes a child whose face, feet, and clothing are left unclean, in the first version by his mother, in the second version by his father. The second vignette is a description of a child who is left unattended after school; in the first case because the mother is consistently late returning from work, in the second instance because of the father's late return. As Table 3 indicates, there is no difference in male and female teachers' use of the abuse label in the case of supervision neglect, even when the gender of the perpetrator is controlled. We might interpret this as an encouraging sign that teachers put equal onus on fathers and mothers to provide their children with adequate after-school care. What is less hopeful is the shift in male teachers' attitudes about neglect of cleanliness. Here, when the perpetrator is the child's mother, almost 75 percent of the men apply the abusive label. Alternatively, when it is the father who is neglecting his child's cleanliness, this

figure drops to just over 50 percent. Apparently, many male teachers tend still to regard mothers as primary caretakers of their children's cleanliness. Besides indicating that they may be more
predisposed toward identifying a child as abused when the mother
seems careless about cleanliness, this implies the perpetuation of
traditional assumptions about family life and an overall tendency to
continue the tradition of blaming mother in cases of neglect
(Health and Welfare Canada, 1989).

Identifying Victims and Reporting Cases

Apart from these significant gender differences, it is worth repeating that teachers overall seem to hold a broad, open-minded set
of definitions when they are thinking theoretically about abuse.
This is important because classroom conditions apparently obscure
all but the most obvious cases. In fact, the findings from this survey
confirm the absolute difficulty of identifying victims under normal
classroom conditions. In this survey, of 336 teachers, only six (less
than 2 percent) said that it is easy to detect the symptoms of sexual
abuse; less than 10 percent indicated that it easy to detect physical
or emotional abuse. About half said that it is easy to pick up on the
indicators of neglect.

The question of why detection is so complicated is partially a
matter of the type of abuse, but it is also clearly tied up in teachers'
focus on children's intellectual development. More than 75 percent of
this sample indicated that they probably would not notice any signs of
sexual abuse *if the child was not having trouble at school.* For physical and emotional abuse, these figures stand at 69 percent and 72 percent, respectively; for neglect, which most teachers seem to feel is
easier to determine than other types of abuse, the figure is a significant 32 percent. This is particularly interesting given the prevailing
assumption that teachers are well-placed to identify child abuse victims and the attention given to the development of the "whole child"
within most educational jurisdictions across the country.

Apart from the central focus on children's learning, it is clear
that classrooms present other complicating conditions. Detecting

physical abuse is difficult, for example, in a setting where large numbers of children present themselves with minor injuries from time to time (82.5 percent of the sample agreed that this a problem), and where abused children can explain away injuries with excuses that sound entirely plausible in their familiarity (79.1 percent). Detecting emotional abuse is difficult in such circumstances as well, since it is not unusual to see a child who seems emotionally distressed in the classroom. In fact, it may be the classroom itself which is at the root of the distress—the difficulties associated with a frustrating math problem, lost homework, or a persistent bully, are just a few that come to mind. It is not hard to imagine how teachers could miss the symptoms of emotional abuse in these circumstances, and in fact more than 70 percent of respondents indicated that this is a difficulty. Most teachers also indicate that emotional distress may be easily mistaken for a medical problem (61.4 percent) or the result of family stress (78.1 percent). Similarly, they point out the difficulty of separating some signs of sexual abuse from the consequences of simply watching too much TV (60.9 percent). Taken together, all of this implies that in the context of a day's work, teachers confront such a wide range of personalities, needs, interests, abilities, and background circumstances, that often only the most extraordinary affairs stand out.

Interpreting children's symptoms in such circumstances requires a very sophisticated knowledge base. Data from earlier studies indicate that most teachers are aware of their legal reporting obligations but are less sure of the signs and symptoms of abuse. Fewer than 40 percent indicated awareness of their school board child abuse policy, and less than half had been required to attend an in-service program. Six years later, the teachers in this study seem only slightly better equipped. The majority (77.1 percent) have received information from their school boards, approximately 60 percent indicate awareness of their school board policy, and 48 percent have attended a mandatory child abuse in-service session in the last five years. Like those in the earlier study, these teachers are not unaware of their training needs, especially in the area of sexual abuse, where 70 percent claim that they are not sufficiently prepared for detecting symptoms. This seems particularly disturbing since more than 80 percent of this sample indicated that children are very unlikely to make disclosures in the case of sexual abuse.

Also troubling is what we might call a continuing professional apprehension about the boundary between physical abuse and appropriate discipline. This shows up in three questionnaire items: two vignettes, the first describing a child who was struck on the face, the second depicting an instance of spanking as discipline for misbehavior; and a statement describing the difficulty of determining physical abuse in a case where an injury may have come about as a consequence of discipline.

Most teachers in this sample applied the abusive label to the facial bruise vignette while approximately a quarter depicted spanking as abusive, implying that for teachers, decisions about physical abuse are clouded by their notions of the necessity for discipline. These uncertainties are reflected in two ways: first in the significant minority of teachers who indicated they were "undecided" about the vignettes (22.4 percent in the case of bruising, 25.7 percent for spanking); and second, in the responses to the statement describing an injury that came about as a result of discipline. For this statement, one of several describing potential detection difficulties, more than a third (37 percent) of the teachers agreed with the idea that detecting physical abuse is difficult when "the injury may have come about as a consequence of a parent's attempts at discipline." This figure replicates the result from the earlier study, which was only slightly higher at 41.7 percent, and implies continuing difficulty with drawing the line between abuse and discipline.

As explained in my analysis of the earlier results (Tite, 1994b), these dilemmas are best understood in the context of contradictory school and criminal code policies with regard to the use of physical force, and against the backdrop of the school's historical association with the application of corporal punishment. These uncertainties also raise questions about the current mood of "getting tough" with students who misbehave at school and indicate that our efforts to curb violence in the school will need to be undertaken with serious attention given to the kinds of messages we wish to put forward about appropriate discipline.

Clearly then, given the school's focus on intellectual development and discipline, the question of how abused children come to their teachers' attention is by no means a simple one. What teachers look for, how much they notice, or what they think about what they see, is neither obvious nor easy to determine. But the conventional wisdom that teachers are well-placed for identifying victims, while glossing over the real difficulties of engaging children on an individual, personal level in the classroom, casts teachers in a role that clearly invites them to ignore all but the most obvious and blatant cases. The results of this survey show that this is probably what is happening.

Just over half of the sampled teachers indicated that they had ever suspected that a child in their class was the victim of child abuse. While I recognize that this analysis needs to go far beyond a simple counting of cases (and I intend to explore the suspicion process more fully in the interview phase), I think a few figures from the survey can provide some interesting background at this stage. The most pertinent measure is the significant gender difference in suspicion, shown in Table 3, that is, 42.7 percent of men teachers compared to 60.1 percent of women teachers indicated that they had suspected a case of abuse. There are two interesting aspects to this gender distinction, the first having to do with the differential effects of men's location in the system, the second pertaining to child abuse policy and in-service training.

First, consider grade level and type of teaching assignment. It makes some sense to assume that teachers who are teaching all subjects in a contained class at the lower grades are better placed for identifying victims than teachers who teach in a specialized area on rotary classes with large numbers of older students. It should be a simple matter of time and opportunity. But the data indicate that grade level has a statistically significant effect on suspicion only for men, and furthermore, in fact, that men teaching all subjects in one contained class are the least likely to indicate suspicion. By contrast, women's suspicion rates are not statistically influenced by grade level or type of class assignment.

Now consider policy and training. Again, we might safely assume that victims might be more easily identified by teachers who are provided with some training about child abuse and its indicators and a clear reporting policy. Certainly, this is the prevailing view in the literature. But the numbers here are very clear—only for women is there is a strong positive correlation between suspicion and in-service training and between suspicion and awareness of policy. Men teachers' indication of suspicion seems unaffected by training and policy.

Table 3
Suspected Abuse—by Gender and Selected Characteristics

| | Male | | Female | | X2 (df) | | |
	n	%	n	%	M	F	Population
All Respondents	53	42.7	122	60.1			9.10 (1)**
By Grade Level					6.04 (2)*		
Kindergarten to							
Grade 6	13	44.8	76	61.3			
Grades 7 to 12	30	37.3	25	52.1			
Combined K to 12	9	75.0	16	66.7			
Teaching Assignment							
Contained Class	7	31.8	71	61.7			6.74 (1)**
Rotary	42	46.2	44	55.7			
Child Abuse In-Service						10.80 (1)**	
At least once	22	46.8	75	70.8			
Never attended	30	40.5	44	47.8			
School Board Policy							
Yes	38	46.3	74	63.2			5.60 (1)*
No, Not sure	15	37.5	45	56.3			

N=327 (124 male, 203 female)
**p. < .01
*p. < .05

By and large, once they have satisfied themselves that they have formed a reasonable suspicion of abuse, women and men teachers tend to proceed in similar ways. As Table 4 indicates, about 85 percent of the women teachers and 75 percent of the men go on to make formal reports, an activity which seems largely independent of other factors, including the type of abuse. Where there is a difference between men and women teachers, it has to do with their awareness of policy; men teachers who indicate no school board policy are the least likely to proceed with a formal report.

There are probably several ways to interpret these figures, but one explanation that seems obvious is that men teachers are simply not as readily prepared as women to engage themselves in the surveillance role. Although it is partially a matter of certain structural

Table 4
Reported Abuse—by Gender and Selected Characteristics

	Male		Female		X2 (df)
	n	%	n	%	Full Popn
As % of All Respondents	40	33.9	103	51.7	9.92 (1)**
As % of Suspected Cases		75.5		84.4	
By Grade Level					
Kindergarten to Grade 6	9	69.2	66	86.8	
Grades 7 to 12	23	76.7	20	80.0	
Combined K to 12	7	77.8	12	75.0	
Type of Teaching Assignment					
Contained Class	5	71.4	63	88.7	
Rotary	32	76.2	33	75.0	
Child Abuse In-Service					
Never attended	23	76.7	34	77.3	
At least once	17	77.3	66	88.0	
Child Abuse Policy					
Yes	32	84.4	65	87.8	
No	8	53.3	36	80.0	4.09 (1)*
Type of Abuse					
Physical Abuse	15	41.7	48	47.5	
Sexual Abuse	16	44.4	33	32.7	
Emotional Abuse	1	2.8	4	4.0	
Neglect	4	11.1	16	15.8	
Age of Victim					
5 to 8	7	18.4	52	50.5	22.36 (3)*
9 to 12	7	18.4	28	27.2	
13 to 16	22	57.9	21	20.4	
Over 16	2	5.3	2	1.9	
Gender of Victim					
Male	15	38.5	47	46.5	
Female	24	61.5	52	51.5	
Both			2	2.0	

N=327, Male = 124, Female = 203   Percentages based on reporters in each category
*p < .05   **p < .01

features like grade level or policy, this is not a sufficient explanation because, as we have seen, these influences pertain mostly to men, and are fairly mixed in any case. What is more likely happening, I would suggest, is a reflection of the fact that gender relations in the school mirror those on the outside (Connell, 1985). Just as the sexual division of labor within education reflects wider work patterns, so teachers' responses to child abuse are likely to reflect men's and women's different understandings, perceptions, and experiences of violence outside of the school.

While there is not enough data in this survey to link teachers' reactions with their personal experiences of violence, there is some emerging evidence in the literature that suggests a connection between professional response to victims and the teacher's gender and personal childhood history of abuse. As an example, Jackson and Nuttall (1993) found that female clinicians in four fields—social work, psychiatry, pediatrics, and psychology—were more apt than men to believe allegations of sexual abuse, and that those who reported a childhood history of abuse were the ones most likely to believe a child's disclosure. In addition, they cite other studies (e.g., Snyder and Newberger, 1986; Attias and Goodwin, 1985; Zellman and Bell, 1990) which show that women tend to judge symptoms of neglect and physical abuse more severely than do men. Similarly, Deblinger and her colleagues (1994) found that women who had strong emotional reactions to child abuse found family counseling too lenient a recommendation in cases of incestuous families. They were more likely to recommend separating victim and perpetrator in such cases. There was no similar divergence between the professional and personal responses for men.

School and Agency Response

To bring this issue into focus, I think we need to acknowledge these distinctions between men's and women's personal attitudes and reactions to abuse, while trying to make sense of how schools give greater legitimacy to men's experience through the handling of questions about suspicious symptoms, and by encouraging particular types of reports and discouraging others. In the schools, few child abuse reports are made without the principals' knowledge. Although there is some procedural variation among school districts, principals are almost always involved, often by conducting their own internal investigations before any outside agency is contacted. Data from the earlier study indicated that fewer than 5 percent of teachers' reports went directly to child welfare agencies without the principals' involvement; in this study, where the provincial policy mandates direct agency reporting, this figure is still a low 15 percent.

While the sample of men teachers is too small to permit a realistic comparison between women and men teachers' reports, it is worth returning briefly to the hypothetical cases described in the vignettes. Table 5 shows the vignette responses for teachers who indicated that they had experienced a situation in their classrooms which seemed similar to the ones described in the vignettes. Though the numbers are small, there is a pattern; about 50 percent of cases are somehow "dropped" at the principals' office, a figure which is consistent with earlier data, and which seems to confirm the low number of referrals made directly to child welfare agencies. Since most principals are male,[2] we will need to look carefully at how principals handle teachers' suspicions, and continue to ask what kinds of reports are encouraged and supported, and why some are waylaid.

But intervention goes beyond the principal's office. Although it is difficult to determine how agencies respond to teachers' reports, the information from this survey indicates that teachers are rarely apprised of the full outcome of their reports. In describing the outcome of cases, less than a third of the reporting teachers stated that their reports resulted in some sort of treatment such as counseling, family support, the removal of the child or the perpetrator from the home, or the laying of criminal charges. Approximately a quarter indicated that their cases were unfounded after the initial investigation. None of the other teachers—representing almost half of the 126 cases described—were able to comment on the full outcome of their reports. By way of explanation, one teacher remarked, "Child Welfare does not report back the results of a teacher's report . . . I guess they would contact the teacher if it was in the best interests of the child." Perhaps. But if we assume that one way of encouraging reports is to follow up teachers' suspicions with a timely investigation and assistance to the abused child, then we will need to ask how this apparent lack of appropriate feedback reinforces the old idea that child abuse is simply not a classroom concern.

Table 5
A Comparison of Mentioning and Reporting Principal and Child Welfare—Vignette Responses

Vignettes	n	Mentioned to Principal %	Reported to Principal %	Reported to Child Welfare %
Bruising	111	64.0	36.0	27.9
Spanking	64	48.4	23.4	18.8
Incest	70	55.7	44.3	38.6
Exposure to pornography	17	52.9	11.8	17.6
Refuse psych treatment	54	72.2	46.3	16.7
Exposure to parents' fighting	92	63.0	23.9	13.0
Neglect cleanliness	190	61.7	24.7	13.2
Neglect supervision	104	51.9	19.2	14.4
Refuse psych-ed testing	75	70.7	41.3	9.3
Refuse vision/ hearing test	48	64.6	39.6	8.3

n = number of teachers who indicated witnessing a case similar to the one described in the vignette: 327 teachers (124 male, 203 female)

Conclusion

By highlighting some of the difficulties associated with coordi-nated action, I have tried to show that we need to focus our attention on the institutional context of systemic violence which gives shape to teachers' reactions to children and to suspicions of child abuse. Al-though that context is not always likely to be consistent, structured into it is a kind of professional consciousness that attends to individ-ual intellectual development and need for discipline, while creating group conditions that obscure all but the most extraordinary cir-cumstances. At another level is the policy context which depends on teachers' knowledge, awareness, and personal attitudes. Gender conflict is built into this, most likely through men and women teachers' differing experiences of violence on the outside, and these difficulties are compounded by their different locations in classrooms and administrative roles. Beyond that, there is a kind of ponderous veil of caution at the agency level which guards against bringing teachers into the heart of the matter. For all the policy and research and talk about involving the schools in the problem, getting people to listen and talk to teachers about child abuse remains mysteriously elusive.

Teachers care about abused children. This is not always obvious because coordinated action is a complex and demanding business. As feminists, we need to start with that and continue to ask about the personal, institutional, and social processes which make it so hard for children to get the help they need.

Notes

1. The research for this paper has been funded by the Social Sciences and Research Council of Canada (File # 410-93-0970). I also wish to acknowledge the Department of Education and Training, Newfoundland and Labrador, for their assistance with the mailing list, and Tish Langlois and Mary Power for helpful comments on earlier drafts of this paper. Thanks also to Cynthia Hicks for assistance with the tables and Margrit Eichler for helpful advice on the questionnaire. An earlier version of this chapter was presented to the Canadian Association for the Study of Women and Education as part of the Canadian Society for the Study of Education Conference in Montreal, Quebec, Canada, June 1995.

2. Canadian figures for 1989–90 indicate that 22 percent of the elementary principals and 8 percent of the secondary principals are female (King and Peart, 1992, p. 146).

References

Abrahams, N., Casey, K., and Daro, D. (1992). Teachers' knowledge, attitudes, and beliefs about child abuse and its prevention. *Child Abuse and Neglect, 16*, 229–38.

Attias, R. and Goodwin, J. (1985). Knowledge and management strategies in incest cases: A survey of physicians, psychologists and family counsellors. *Child Abuse and Neglect, 9*, 527–533.

Beck, K., Ogloff, J. and Corbishley, A. (1994). Knowledge, compliance, and attitudes of teachers toward mandatory child abuse reporting in British Columbia. *Canadian Journal of Education, 19* (1), 15–29.

Cole, S. (1985). Child battery. In C. Guberman and M. Wolfe (Eds.), *No safe place: Violence against women and children* (pp. 21–40). Toronto: Women's Press.

Connell, R. (1985). *Teachers' work*. North Sydney, Australia: George Allen & Unwin Publishers Ltd.

Deblinger, E., Lippmann, J., Stauffer, L. and Finkel, M. (1994). Personal versus professional responses to child sexual abuse allegations. *Child Abuse and Neglect, 18* (8), 679–82.

Government of Newfoundland and Labrador (1993). *Provincial child abuse policy and guidelines.* St. John's: Government of Newfoundland and Labrador, Department of Education, Division of Student Support Services.

Health and Welfare Canada. (1989). *Family violence: A review of theoretical and clinical literature.* Ottawa: Health and Welfare Canada.

Herzberger, S. D. (1988). Cultural obstacles to the labeling of abuse by professionals. In A. Maney and S. Wells (Eds.), *Professional responsibilities in protecting children: A public approach to child sexual abuse* (pp. 33–44). New York: Praeger Publishers.

Jackson, H. and Nuttall, R. (1993). Clinician responses to sexual abuse allegations. *Child Abuse and Neglect, 17*, 127–143.

King, A. J. C. and Peart, M. J. (1992). *Teachers in Canada: Their work and quality of life.* Ottawa: Canadian Teachers' Federation.

Maher, P. (Ed). (1987). *Child abuse: The educational perspective.* Oxford: Basil Blackwell.

Maney. A. (1988). Professional involvement in public health strategies for the prevention and control of child sexual abuse. In A. Maney and S. Wells (Eds.), *Professional responsibilities in protecting children: A public approach to child sexual abuse* (pp. 3–22). New York: Praeger Publishers.

Mahony, P. (1989). Who pays the price? Sexual abuse and education. *Gender and Education, 1* (1), 87–91.

McEvoy, A. B. (1990). Child abuse law and school policy. *Education and Urban Society*, *22* (3), 247–57.

McIntyre, T. (1990). The teachers' role in cases of suspected child abuse. *Education and Urban Society*, *22* (3), 300–306.

Snyder, J. C. and Newberger, E. H. (1986). Consensus and difference among hospital professionals in evaluating child maltreatment. *Violence and Victims*, *1* (2), 125–39.

Tite, R. (1993). How teachers define and respond to child abuse: The distinction between theoretical and reportable cases. *Child Abuse and Neglect*, *17*, 591–603.

Tite, R. (1994a). Muddling through: The procedural marginalization of child abuse. *Interchange*, *25* (1), 87–108.

Tite, R. (1994b). Detecting the symptoms of child abuse: Classroom complications. *Canadian Journal of Education*, *19* (1), 1–14.

Zellman, G. (1990). Linking schools and social services: The case of child abuse reporting. *Educational Evaluation and Policy Analysis*, *12* (1), 41–55.

Zellman, G. and Bell, K. (1989). *The role of professional background, case characteristics, and protective agency response in mandated child abuse reporting*. Santa Monica, CA: Rand Corporation.

Part II

Systemic Violence in Pedagogical Practice

Chapter 4

Opening Spaces:
Examining the Blocks[1]

Pam Whitty

Block play as a form of social, imaginative, and constructive play has the potential to help children learn the traditional 3Rs as well as the 3Cs of care, concern and connection named by Jane Roland Martin (1985). According to Martin (1994), the quality of life in schools needs to "command the foreground" so that questions are asked about classroom routines and rituals as well as relationships amongst teachers and children and children themselves. This chapter examines how a classroom routine of "choice" during "free play" brought about a "rule" that excluded girls from the block area. The uncovering of this rule illuminates how rituals of play can prevent some children from access to specified curricular materials and opportunities and may describe a "learning experience" in which children take on dominant and submissive roles based on gender.

Education in the "Problems of Life"

In 1912, when Helen Keller was thirty-two, she advised women to make the "problems of life" the source of educational endeavors (Keller, 1920), or, as we might say in the current historical moment, make the familiar problematic. In kindergarten classrooms, the gendered landscapes of the play preferences of girls and

59

boys are taken for granted. It is this kind of familiarity that Keller calls us to examine.

Research on the play preferences of girls and boys during free play in preschool educational settings indicates that the preferred activities of girls include small group interactions, generally confined in space and physical movement. Most boys, on the other hand tend to engage in group activities that require physical movement in a larger nonrestrictive area (Liss, 1986). Over time, most girls demonstrate a preference for house play and doll play, though preference for the latter was found to be diminishing in more recent studies (Liss, 1986; Sutton-Smith and Rosenberg, 1971). Generally, girls also prefer scissors, paints, paper, art and conversation play while boys prefer transportation toys, sandbox play, blocks and construction toys, and rough and tumble play. Girls more often engage in unstructured fantasy play and cooperative games while boys are involved in competitive, hierarchical games (Mackie, 1991). However, in an analysis of preferred games and activities among boys and girls from 1896 to 1959, "the responses of girls have become increasingly like those of boys . . . the boys' roles have become increasingly circumscribed" (Sutton-Smith and Rosenberg, 1971, p. 48).

How is it that we come to take children's preferences and their embodiments for granted? Social markers such as children's names, clothing, books, games, and toys are ways through which children learn about gendered expectations from the moment of birth or, if the sex of the child is known, before birth (Delamont, 1990). By age four, preschoolers are "strongly influenced by societal norms for gender behavior and accept that girls and boys are supposed to do different things" (Derman Sparkes, 1989). Indeed, children's beliefs about how girls and boys ought to act often prevail over their own experience. It comes as no surprise then, that by the time of school entry, "young children have already developed specific notions about differences between boys and girls" (Bailey, 1993). Nor is it surprising that pedagogies of play, and free play in particular, provide opportunities for children to reproduce and negotiate gendered relations of power (Walkerdine, 1990).

In this chapter, I write about a series of "conversational moments," an idea I borrow from feminist philosopher Elisabeth Young-Bruehl (1987). The conversational moments I bring together demonstrate how one boy's agenda in a kindergarten classroom became visible to the students I teach, the teacher, and myself. As you will read, the children, and some of their parents, were aware of a specifically gendered curriculum and the dynamics by which it was being created and maintained.

Conversational Moments as Consciousness Raising

Blocks, and in particular unit blocks, have been a part of early childhood classrooms in North America for almost one hundred years. Initially used in programs for young children in settlement houses in New York City, Caroline Pratt's blocks eventually became standard equipment in her own school and then across North America. Block play provides an aesthetic and integrative means of learning for young children as they construct, imagine, and reconstruct and reimagine the various social, physical, and emotional worlds they inhabit. Further, children, through their interactions with blocks and each other, have multiple opportunities to learn and practice aspects of mathematics, science, language, social studies, and geography (Hirsch, 1984; Sprague Mitchell, 1934/91; Reifel and Yeatman, 1991).

For thirteen years I worked in a variety of settings including day care, kindergarten, first grade, and special education. I was often surprised by the things I learned directly from the children and visitors to the classroom. Children and visitors, whether the visitors be other children, student interns, parents or other professionals, noticed things which I did not. Their place and role in the classroom world I had created with the children was different from my own. As such, the observations and comments made by others raised my consciousness to aspects of the various classroom curricula that may otherwise have remained hidden to me. Now, in the university classroom, I find that similar surprises continue to reveal the taken-for-granted.

An undergraduate class I teach in early childhood curriculum has a weekly practicum requirement in local kindergarten settings. One day a surprising question was asked by a student teacher. Why is there a "no-girls-in-the-blocks" rule? The student who posed the question had been told, emphatically, by four girls that no girls were allowed in the blocks. When she asked them why, the reply was "the boys said so." The teacher of the kindergarten class where the conversation had taken place, was surprised to learn of the existence of this rule. It is the history and origin of this "rule" that I have made the topic of this deconstruction.

Who are "the boys" and "the girls" in any particular class? Thorne (1994) proposes that when gender boundaries are activated, "the loose aggregation 'boys and girls' becomes 'the boys' and 'the girls' as separate and reified groups" (p. 65). In this case, the acceptance by these four girls of a no-girls-in-the-blocks rule signified the activation of a specific gender boundary, a boundary these girls would not cross even with the encouragement of a pre-service teacher.

One of the very real teaching dilemmas in this particular classroom was the number of children in the class, and the ratio of boys to girls: fifteen children—five girls and ten boys. The teacher was aware that the girls were rarely in the block area; however, she attributed this, in part, to the fact that there were so few girls and that in previous years girls tended to enter the block area later in the year. Although children's choices changed over the course of the year, the subtleties of shifting spaces remained to be examined.

Shortly after the teacher had been made aware of the no-girls rule, she encountered it directly and took action. Her story:

> It was first thing in the morning and four girls were standing in the block area looking around. Usually one or two of the boys arrived first and went directly to the blocks. However, no boys were here yet so the girls had gone over. When I saw them standing there I went over and suggested that they build with the blocks. No, they said, they weren't allowed to play in the blocks. When I asked them why they thought that, they said "the boys said so." I told them "I don't think so," and began taking the interconnecting blocks off the shelves. The unit blocks were mostly in use from a structure that had been built the previous day, so we used these ones. When I did this the girls joined in with me. From this time forward these girls did enter the block area of the classroom. However, as I discovered later, there were specific ways they used the blocks and specific blocks they used. A short time later I had a conversation with a few of the kindergarten boys and I learned two things about gender and block play in this particular class-

room. First, "the girls make houses and the boys make army buildings," and secondly, "the boys" played with "balance" blocks (unit blocks) and "the girls" played with the "attach-it" blocks (interconnecting planks)." Initially when I asked for an elaboration on the gendered differences, I was told "it's just what we do" (teacher's personal journal).

According to the teacher, the boy who apprised me of the gender differentiation was well respected as a leader in the classroom. He told me that the balance blocks were much harder to work with than the attach-it blocks. He explained his point with direct references to an army building. He made repeated verbal mention to balance as he touched pivotal blocks whose removal would result in the collapse of the entire building. When two other boys, who were also explaining their views, said they sometimes played with the attach-it blocks, the other boy declared, adamantly, that he never did. The two boys who played with the attach-it blocks, as it turned out, were also the two who most often played with children of both sexes.

When I shared this particular series of conversational moments with the teacher, she added another insight. She wondered if one set of blocks was any more difficult than the other or if the value of the blocks had been assigned by the influential boy. From my perspective, such an interpretation might mean "the girls' blocks" were being constructed as being of less working/playing value than "the boys' blocks." Whatever interpretation might be applied, the blocks clearly had been assigned varying degrees of difficulty, related to sex, by this influential boy. He was actively constructing gender for himself and for the other children in the classroom.

As our informal conversations continued, the teacher had another significant encounter with the influential boy in which she observed this boy's power over other members of the class, both boys and girls. In response to a child's experience with day surgery and a subsequent class field trip to the nursing faculty, the teacher had redesigned the house corner for hospital play. When the influential boy and two others approached the area and were invited in, the influential boy said "No way!" He walked away. Two other boys left with him. Sensing that the other boys wanted to play in the hospital area, the teacher encouraged one to be an ambulance driver and eventually, the influential boy was drawn in, at which time he took more and more control of the play, giving orders and directions and creating accident scenarios. The girls, not incidentally, initially took on the role of patients before they were willing to become the doctors. The teacher stayed with the play the entire time.

Meanwhile, I had a conversation with the mother of one of the boys. This mother had noticed that her son had stopped playing with the girls in the classroom; however, when he went to day care after class, he played with the very girls that he ignored in the kindergarten setting. From her son, this mother learned that one of the boys in the kindergarten had said that they were not to play with the girls. Another mother noticed that since her daughter had come to kindergarten, she had stopped playing with her blocks at home nor did she play with them at school. In both cases, the mothers were deeply concerned about their children's movement towards what they viewed as stereotypical gendered play preferences; the mothers mediated the situation through talk and deliberate actions at home.

This classroom, where the no-girls rule was created, was homogeneous in terms of race and class, specifically white and middle class. The gender boundary in the blocks emerged as one site of dominance. In this case, one influential boy, for a period of time until the rule was exposed, was able to keep girls out of the blocks and to convince some boys to do likewise. Once the teacher became aware of what was taking place, she began to alter the relations of power by opening the block area to everyone and by attending to and entering play in other areas of the room. In Ruth Goodenough's studies of kindergartens (1987), she noted that dominance by one male child can set the tone for the other boys and draw them into contempt for girls. Such appears to be the case with the no-girls rule. Some of the boys and all of the girls were subjected to one boy's growing understanding and enactment of his emerging masculinity. This young boy's understanding of what it meant to be a boy included keeping girls out of the blocks, defining the materials that boys played with as inherently more valued, refusing to play with the blocks the girls played with, and convincing some of the boys that they need not play with girls at all. What the girls were learning, in part, was to accept male authority that excluded them from access to particular materials, materials that dominated a large part of the floor space in this classroom, materials that held the potential for numerous social, intellectual, physical, and aesthetic learning opportunities.

Questioning Classroom Routines, Rituals, and Relationships

How is Helen Keller's "modern woman" to respond to this enactment of masculine authority in a kindergarten setting? What are the broader lessons to be learned from these conversational moments? To abandon pedagogies of play would be an extreme response. As teachers, educators, parents, and children we must make ourselves aware of what is problematic about play pedagogies, particularly in terms of power relations. We need to question and examine, as Martin (1992) suggests, our classroom routines, rituals, and relationships. We also must question the idea and practice, as Walkerdine (1990) does, of leaving "natural, normal children" alone to develop on their own. Natural, normal children are subjected to and constructed by the social context of their lives. As teachers we need to become aware of the real power of rules and relationships that become authoritarian.

We might start with questioning the daily, weekly, yearly routines of our classrooms and consider what choice means in the context of a classroom. Who is choosing what, when, with whom, and under what circumstances? When children are making choices about which areas of the room they will occupy and what activities will engage them, we need to ask, are these choices open to them and others, later in the day, the week, the month, the year? When does daily continued presence in an area mean that it "belongs" to a certain group of people? Does physical, spatial dominance translate to other forms of dominance? Is, for example, a boy's control of space, as Thorne (1994) suggests, anticipating "a pattern of claimed entitlement, perhaps linked to patterns well documented in adults" (p. 83)?

Courage and Curiosity in Teaching

Opening up spaces in play-based classrooms is likely to take different forms for different teachers and groups of children. In this case, the kindergarten teacher paid careful attention to who was in what area of the room over extended periods of time and disrupted a routine that had become a ritual for a group of boys through the occupation of a particular space. This physical claim apparently dissuaded other children, whom she named as less assertive children, female and male, from entering the block area. She was able to alter the routine by ensuring that other members of the class had the opportunity to enter the blocks and by encouraging these boys to explore other areas of the room. Now she speaks directly with the children when she notices that particular recurring choices may be creating or illuminating inequities. It sometimes takes courage to speak, which is not surprising considering the strength of societal expectations and the unexpected anger of some young boys when relations of power between the children are disrupted or interrupted by the teacher.

Speaking directly with children about the taken-for-granted, while respecting their views and their understandings of the world, is a pedagogical approach that other teachers also practice. For example, when Gorham (1994) noticed that for several weeks no girls in his kindergarten classroom were involved in the main ongoing activity in the room, namely the constructing, painting, and dramatization of bus making, he wondered why:

> Up to this point, bus making had been primarily a boys' project, although girls had watched buses being made and had played as passengers. As I collected the buses one day, I wondered why no girls had yet made a bus. A discussion with some girls and boys after school, while we were waiting for the buses, revealed that everyone thought driving a bus was a boys' thing to do. Patrick was quite sure of this, even though the bus that brings him to school is driven by a woman. Within a few days of the conversation, several girls started to make buses. These buses were different; the girls painted the fronts a bright school bus yellow and painted in the details that Patrick and his crew would have drawn on with markers. Kylie made a bus complete with grill, headlights and red flashers (Gorham, 1994, p. 9–10).

The kindergarten teacher deliberately pointed out paradoxes to the children to see how they would respond and to make their thinking visible. The children responded stereotypically about who drives buses, but it may well be that the teacher's illumination of the paradox encouraged some of the girls to enter the bus making space in their own unique way. Jane Roland Martin (1994) suggests that a "small act of courage" (p. 241) might begin to transform the curriculum and make gender a subject entity in public schools. Where the first kindergarten teacher's actions clearly speak to Martin's recognition of the significance of small acts of courage, the second case suggests that small acts of curiosity may also create new possibilities.

As a teacher-educator I have found that courage and curiosity sometimes interact in the form of questions. One of the more powerful examples of a single question making a significant difference comes from my work with Sherry Billings, a second-grade teacher. As a participant-observer in her classroom, I took field notes, and turned the notes back to her, sometimes with a question or two. My particular question on this occasion emerged from my note-taking of a twenty-two-minute group time. I was struck by the child-led nature of the group, the attentiveness of the children listening to other children, and the teacher's role as an active listener rather than facilitator of the conversation. My question was: How do you ensure equity during this verbal sharing time?

That question ignited Sherry, and from it she began her own investigation. In her desire for concrete evidence about who participated in group sharing time, she decided to open up the verbal space by providing request forms for those who wished to speak. Here is what she discovered:

> After three weeks I sorted the requests and discovered girls' requests outnumbered boys by 7 to 1. For me this imbalance raised two questions: was a written request the only way most girls and a few boys could be guaranteed an opportunity to speak in the large group and/or was the style of request, written and private, more conducive to particular children (Billings and Whitty, 1994, p. 7)?

The teacher continued her investigation and was "disturbed" to find numerous imbalances in her classroom. She found differences between girls and boys and amongst girls and boys, for example, in the ability to persevere in mathematical games, in who chose to bake, in who participated in what physical activities on the playground and in the gymnasium, and in who cleaned the classroom.

Sherry, like the teacher in the "no-girls-in-the-blocks" case, noticed that, over the course of the year, different children engaged in different classroom activities. She taught these children for first and second grade and over the two-year period she noticed a shift in the play/work focus of the children. Specifically she saw an increasing tendency for the children to sex-segregate and a growing disdain on the part of some of the boys to engage with girls. The girls, she noted, were more subtle about their preferences. The teacher also learned something about her own differing actions with different children. She noticed that she related most easily to the more assertive rather than the less assertive children. Generally speaking, this meant that she interacted most often with a group of boys and one girl, the only girl to cross what Thorne (1994) refers to as the gender divide.

Re-Searching Our Actions

My actions and interactions with teachers at various levels, continue to raise questions about the role of sex-segregated spaces in the context of coeducational classrooms. Do we need to consider separate education rather than coeducation for children in the early years of schooling? Would this be for all of the time, or for some of the time? What would be the content of that education? What would we learn by so doing?

These questions have been considered by Britt-Marie Berge (1995) and her colleagues at Umea University, Sweden who are engaged in a three-year study they call Equitypedagogy. Working with eleven teachers, seven female and four male, and their seven-to-thirteen-year-old students, they seek to make explicit, enact, and observe the need for pedagogical development inside and outside the classroom.

Although the project is a cooperative one between university researchers and classroom teachers, the more formal action research project evolved from the observations of one female teacher who was examining the context of her own classroom. The teacher began to separate the pupils into single-sex groups during 20 to 25 percent of class hours because she had noticed that boys were dominating the classroom. She wanted to break the boys' domination and to strengthen the influence of the girls. She persuaded the other teachers to join her, even if they did not share the same experience of boys' domination in the classroom. After three years, the teachers wanted to get feedback and develop their pedagogy, so they initiated an action research project (Berge, 1995).

This project grew from the observations and actions of a single teacher in an elementary school. Her actions speak to the power of the teacher, her observation of inequities in her own educational setting, and the positive effects of joining with other advocating adults to work towards equity for children. Equal access does not equal equity. Equity pedagogy, a major component in realizing equity, includes small acts of courage and/or curiosity by a few people in a particular educational setting. I trust this chapter indicates that small acts can have large consequences and that respectful conversations among adults and children, and adults and adults can encourage thoughtful change. Working toward equity between females and males is a challenging and energizing task as we continue to educate ourselves, as Helen Keller would say, in the circumstances of our own lives.

Note

1. With thanks to the teachers who contributed to this work, Pam Wister, Peter Gorham, and Sherry Billings. An earlier version of this chapter was presented to the Canadian Association for the Study of Women and Education as part of the Canadian Society for the Study of Education Conference in Calgary, Alberta, Canada, June 1994.

References

Bailey, K. (1993). *The girls are the ones with the pointy nails.* London, Ontario: Althouse Press.

Berge, B.-M. (1995, May). *Equity pedagogy.* Paper presented at the Third Annual Madison Wisconsin Action Research Network Conference, Madison, WI.

Billings, S. and Whitty, P. (1994, June). Critical conflicts with self. A paper presented at Early Childhood Research Association Conference. Calgary, AB.

Delamont, S. (1990). *Sex roles and the school.* London: Routledge.

Derman Sparkes, L. (1989). *Anti-bias curriculum.* Washington, DC: National Association for the Education of Young Children.

Goodenough, R. (1987). Small group culture and the emergence of sexist behavior: A comparative study of four children's groups. In G. Spindler and L. Spindler (Eds.), *Interpretive ethnology of Communication.* Hillsdale: J. Lawrence Erlbaum.

Gorham, P. (1994). Bus 21. In M. Leavitt and P. Whitty (Eds.), *The living curriculum.* Fredericton, N.S.: Queen's Printer.

Hirsch, E. (1984). *The block book.* Washington, DC: National Association for the Education of Young Children.

Keller, H. (1920). *Out of the dark.* New York: Doubleday.

Liss, M. (1986). The young child at play. In G. Fein and M. Rivkin (Eds.), *Reviews of research: Vol. 4* (pp. 127–39). Washington, DC: National Association for the Education of Young Children.

Mackie, M. (1991). *Gender relations in Canada.* Toronto: Butterworths.

Martin, J. R. (1985). *Reclaiming a conversation: The ideal of the educated woman.* New Haven: Yale University Press.

Martin, J. R. (1992). *The schoolhome: Rethinking schools for changing families.* Cambridge: Harvard University Press.

Martin, J. R. (1994). *Changing the educational landscape: Philosophy, women and curriculum.* New York: Routledge.

Ramsey, P. (1991). *Social dynamics of early childhood making friends in school: Promoting peer relationships in early childhood.* New York: Teachers College.

Reifel S., and Yeatman, J. (1991). Action, talk and thought in block play. In B. Scales, M. Almy, A. Nicolopoulou and S. Ervin-Tripp (Eds.), *Play and the social context of development in early care and education.* New York: Teachers College.

Sprague Mitchell, L. (1934/91) *Young geographers: How they ex-plore the worlds and how they map their world* (Anniversary Edition). New York: Bank Street College of Education.

Sutton-Smith, B., and Rosenberg, R.G. (1971). Sixty years of histor-ical change in the game preferences of American children. In R. E. Herron and B. Sutton-Smith (Eds). *Child's Play* (pp. 18–50). New York: John Wiley & Sons.

Thorne, B. (1994). *Gender play: Girls and boys in school.* New Brunswick, NJ: Rutgers University Press.

Walkerdine, V. (1990). *Sex, power and pedagogy: Schoolgirl fictions.* London: Venso.

Young-Bruehl, E. (1987). The education of women as philosophers. *Signs, 12* (2). 35–49.

Chapter 5

Video Games:
Playing on a
Violent Playground[1]

Linda Wason-Ellam

It is evident from the previous chapter that children learn social constructions through play and social networks. Do they also learn to be violent when the play they engage in is based on violent play themes? Childhood themes for violent play are drawn from real life and from fantasy. Classical fairy tales, movies, video games, and television provide many violent themes, while others may come from actual violence the children may witness. Antagonists, whether they be robbers, monsters, witches, or super heroes, may change with time, but the role consistently revolves around acts of dominance and submission. Aggressive play based on these themes results in someone who is more powerful being a "winner" and someone who is weaker being "defeated." Sometimes, the play has a pro-social theme, such as rescuing people or property from evil, but often the basic message is that violent weapons or methods can be effective in solving problems.

The documented roles of violent, aggressive acts to which children are being exposed in play have received increased attention from educators and policy makers as these acts have transgressed boundaries and become more prevalent in school. Huesmann (1994) asserts that the media has played a key role in desensitizing our society to systemic violence in such a way that it is now considered to be culturally normative. Teachers are becoming aware that children's play is often imitative of video game super heroes, such as Shredder, Krang, Raphael, or Baxter, and reflects an intense need for young children to act out in hostile and violent ways or "combat play" (Hicks, 1992; Gronlund, 1992).

Combat play, which is entrenched in strong character identification, stresses the internalization and recasting of video game scripts with aggressive, macho and stylized actions. Some school districts report that an increasing number of children bring kitchen knives to school "just in case," while acting out violent scripts during recess time. These circumstances call into question the apparent hegemony of media scripts and the traditional wisdom about playing with violence. To understand the complexities of violent media play within a social context, I present in this chapter an in-depth account of a socially isolated grade two video game player who simulates the violent and aggressive play and actions of the game's super heroes throughout his classroom talk and writing. The specificity of this narrative makes this text an act of political intervention, consciously chosen by me to create a moment of transformation.

Violence with a Pen

What is the context for understanding children and violence? Usually, it is precipitated in social acts where children engage in overt conflict. However, it may be occurring covertly embedded within the context of classroom learning as is the case of Duc Lan, who engaged in simulated violence in a variety of literacy learning activities. For example, his teacher attempted to create an atmosphere in which children had the freedom to choose their own topics and write for those who mattered—themselves, their classmates, parents, siblings, and friends. The teacher began with the recognition that each individual came to the writing workshop with concerns, ideas, memories, and feelings that needed to be shared (Calkins, 1986). The teacher's role was to listen and to help the writers listen to the voices inside themselves, for school was a place where ideas were valued and respected (Giroux, 1983).

Within this framework, writing was a cooperative effort, as the children were encouraged to talk to others about their drafts. It was an exhilarating, noncompetitive, and enriching experience for many of the young writers who wrote at length as they revised and edited in an atmosphere of acceptance and respect. But that was not always the case. Some children like Duc Lan, an ESL (English as a Second Language) student, enjoyed exploring topics that may be daring but were not always appropriate for sharing with others:

(Field Note Excerpt): Tethering his thoughts during writers' workshop, Duc Lan is clandestinely hunched over with his pen to the paper as he begins to replicate the serial plot and violent action garnered from playing the latest weekend video game rental. His depersonalized text, reflects a lack of authentic voice since video game topics such as violence and combative tactics were not for class consumption and he was interested in little else. For Duc Lan, his concept of writing was "verbal tailoring from ready-made cloth," a media narrative. For some, reworking video material can be seen as a form of parody or a post-modern form of pastiche, but for him it was a form of recasting the media voice.

Grifter saw two robots. They opened fire. He pulled his two guns out and shot both! Boom! Boom! They were both destroyed. He saw another robot with a gun. He went closer. The robot opened fire. Grifter was faster. BLAM! The robot was down. He saw a cartridge. He picked it up, then went on. When Grifter saw the energy generator he put the cartridge in and powered it to fifty. Grifter went back and saw the cartridge generator. He put the cartridge in and a bridge appeared. A robot came from in front and Grifter blew it away. ZAP! "Got you, Dude!" Grifter went back to the generator and there was an elevator. He walked up and a jungle man shot Grifter. But Grifter has a healing factor. Grifter shot! BLAM! BLAM!

When the classroom teacher draws near to monitor his progress with an on-the-spot conference, Duc Lan scrunches the paper and quickly discontinues composing the graphic details of the video story. He pulls out his writer's journal and pens a routine entry about a more acceptable theme, "his own lived experiences"—a trip to the local supermarket.

The Supermarket

I go to the store with my mom and my sister. We buy juice and crackers. That's all that was good to eat. The end.

Another journal entry, another prosaic topic that puts little demand upon Duc Lan's literacy ability; rather than writing, he just puts down words, following other words. The teacher dismissed the minimal entry because of his ESL status. She believed that a beginning writer needed time to work out his ideas. What the teacher never saw were the other elaborated texts recast from video scripts brimming with gory details that were stuffed into his workspace just waiting to be shared with his peers. Frequently, he pulled out these daring texts and read them to eager classmates. Why? Perhaps he did it for the recognition or as a way to show his skill as a video game player since ability as a game player may equal self-worth:

The Killer

One day a little girl was missing! They looked all the world. Until they looked under a bed. Oh my god! said the wife.

The girl was on the floor. She was dead! She had a nife in her tummy!"

Entering the Classroom Culture

Duc Lan, "a latchkey child" (his parents worked shifts), was a member of a grade two multilingual classroom that I entered on a voyage of discovery, hoping to understand the social-cultural context of school literacy. While viewing his daily interaction in literacy events, I was able to go beyond the snapshot of classroom life to uncover what lies beneath—the social reality of the school culture which is composed of many layers. I was able to fit together the puzzle pieces of Duc Lan's leisure time—the forty plus hours per week of compulsive play within the video game world of simulated combat maneuvers. Video games filled a social and cultural gap within his home space and provided him with companionship. This high-tech domain served as his breakfast entertainment as well as his afternoon and evening ritual during the hours he was home alone. It provided a means of intensifying his everyday culture and a way of escaping it. It only became problematic in school when he incorporated its language and themes into his expression of ideas. Thus, the popularity of video games and their violent cultural form raise significant questions about how game playing structures young audiences and impacts upon their literacies.

During a sabbatical year, I joined an elementary classroom community as Linda, "an honorary classmate." In this persona, I had hoped to understand literacy in a multilingual classroom. My intent was to listen to the voices of those who are generally silenced or whose presence is partially invisible to those who, like me, dwell in the privilege of age, class, or gender. I asked myself what literacy might look like if I chose to direct my attention to matters generally obscured by my ordinary habits of thought, dispositions, and categories. Using this framework, I challenged myself by moving from the role of "adultcentric observer" (Hubbard, 1989, p. 11–13), sketching what I thought was happening in classrooms, to one in which "I immersed myself in the social lives of the children." Like Fuller (1984), Neilsen (1989), and Mies (1991), who entered into the lives of their informants, I became a participating member of the grade two culture. I came to learn that children themselves are culture transformers and creators.

Seated at tables and work areas, I joined these learners as a critical friend, an arrangement that allowed me to connect to the classroom culture. By dialoguing, writing, reading aloud, collaborating, listening, observing, story making, I interacted with patience and without imposing. Outside on the playground I was a "keener," taking part in jump rope, freeze tag, kick ball, and other games while at the same time remaining immersed in the interactions and language. Sometimes, after school hours, I was invited to classmates' homes or birthday celebrations which helped me understand how families spent their leisure time. To me, traditional educational research has been like "seeing around corners," that is, literacy learning has been observed from an angled view looking at what children are doing and producing rather than discovering the contexts in which this learning occurs. I assumed an emic perspective or insider's view of reality (Watson-Gegeo, 1988) to consider the influence of social context on literacy activity and to access information across a variety of frameworks. In ethnographic inquiry, "observations are contextualized, both in the immediate setting in which behavior is observed and in further contexts beyond that context" (Spindler and Spindler, 1987, p. 18). In this stance, I could not tell in advance where the moments of truth would be, nor could I plan ahead because I did not know what might be possible and where the connections eventually would lead. From my vantage point, I was able to view the intersection of a number of literacies including the connecting of writing, talk, and video game scripts.

Questioning carries an assumptive nature and cultural baggage (Tamivarra and Enright, 1986). Therefore, I chose to be conversational in my interactions with the children rather than bombarding them with a shopping list of questions. In my day-to-day encounters, I suggested that I was uninformed and made statements to the children such as, "I am not sure, I don't think I know, or can you help me to understand this?" Assuming this posture was not just a manipulative tool, it was a way of conceding power to try to see literacy from the children's situated view. The tenor of the classroom was one of learners who were eager to teach me as ethnographic informants. I kept a record of my time with the children through field notes and my daily journal.

Many of these recollections are focused on Duc Lan's obsession with video games and their cult heroes. Duc Lan was a loner who rarely participated with others in classroom chat or playground games. I defined his behavior as anti-social—hostile to the well-being of society and aversive to others (Walker, Colvin, and Ramsay, 1994). I became Duc Lan's friend by default as he had no other companions in the classroom community with whom he could discuss his interests. It was during these intimate moments of school life that I observed interactions and patterns of behavior about his "adulation of video games" and his lack of interest in literacy activities such as reading stories or writing. Eventually, I observed other young boys (seven grade two boys and four grade three boys) who spent much of their after-school time in the microworlds of video games. In all cases, it appeared that part of the appeal of video scripts was the boys' need to exert power and control over their environments, even though that power and control may be in a limited arena.

Video Games as Rule-Governed Playgrounds

As an electronic literacy, video game playing has soared into popularity and become a part of the culture of childhood and youth (Soper, 1993). According to Provenzo (1991), video games are the fusion of media; they are riding on the technological cusp of puzzle-solving computer games and strategy games minus the social interaction. Video game playing is a linear goal-oriented path compared to the imaginative worlds hatched from play with storybooks, or less scripted play such as Legos, dollhouses, cars, and trucks. Provenzo (1991) cautions that excessive video playing can be isolating as it prevents young viewers from engaging in more interactive, imaginative or problem-solving activities. He believes that video games allow children little or no freedom to make decisions for themselves, to weave their own fantasies and in turn their own mysteries. There is only one path down which a video game player can proceed. In contrast, pretend worlds like those created by toys or literature allow children to create their own paths for they are still in control of their play.

Bettelheim (1987) states that one of the most important functions of play and games for a child is a chance "to experiment with various roles and forms of social interaction in order to determine the suitability for himself" (p. 34). Video games may influence the social contexts of play for Duc Lan. A child who engages excessively in solitary fantasy play may not be learning the social skills or emotional adjustments necessary for working in a classroom learning community. Duc Lan had incorporated this game-playing culture, its reference points and metaphors into his "self." He was extending it into his talk, reading and writing engagements, and work with others. In some ways, it was overshadowing his full immersion in classroom literacy. This then, becomes a thorny issue: Who has agency over the imaginary ideas in children's play? Is game playing just a spectator sport or does active participation allow players to step into a new type of electronic literacy that inspires the simulation of aggressive language and behaviors?

According to Provenzo (1991), video games are a struggle for survival. One does not have to understand; all that is required is just to make the right moves. The player can either follow the rules exactly or lose the game. Success is measured in how skillfully a player can assault an endless battery of opponents by mustering potent weapons. Unlike literary or imaginary worlds, the almost hypnotic fascination of video games is the idea of rule-governed fantasy worlds filled with blatant aggression and violence. Video game makers claim that video games encourage planning, estimating, and higher level thinking skills. A bonus attraction is winning or achieving a high score. This may not be so. Video game playing may be an action-addiction. A good memory and a fast finger go a long way. Nodelman (1990) states that "victory or defeat depends upon manual dexterity" (p. 47). Video game playing requires quick thinking as a player is continually challenged to act and do. Things must happen instantaneously; if you stop to think while playing, you lose. There is no time to reflect, only to adapt.

However, with total concentration, this fantasy world can be controlled. And in turn, it can *control the player*. The rules are preset and fixed, rather than negotiated as there can be no dialogue with absent game designers. Instead, learning the rules becomes the game. There is no critical thinking because there is no opportunity to have input, analyze, or have a personal response. Therefore, the status quo wins every time if the player follows what has already been designed. If there is no opportunity to change the game, no negotiation, then the player is merely memorizing the rules. One needs to consider the social consequences of training children to follow the rules unquestionably so they can win.

Videos as a Talking Toy

As a cultural form, the popular video games such as Nintendo's Super Mario and Teenage Mutant Ninja Turtles are fueled and guided by commercial enterprises which have swayed the consumer marketplace with Nintendo merchandise reaping a whopping profit. Canny promotional strategies have marketed an enticing array of "must have" paraphernalia such as watches, clothes, lunch kits, dolls, wallpaper, bedding, and cereal, all of which help children assume the social codes and traditions based on the Nintendo games and characters. Rather than remain just consumer products they embellish a "back story" (Kline, 1993, p. 212), a narrative, that carries a character profile within an imaginary but familiar world. It provides children with ideas or a script about themselves and the culture they live in. From observations in Duc Lan's classroom, children sporting Nintendo goods had ample opportunities to enact and assume the back story with its aggressive language and actions in daily classroom and playground interplays.

Kinder (1991) conceptualizes video games as "talking toys," for they provide a child with a powerful means of "reenvoicing cultural values" (p. 22). Borrowing from Bakhtin's theory of dialogism, she explains reenvoicement as an intertextual process which mediates between imitation—a mere repetition of what is heard—and sentence creativity, where new combinations are generated. Accordingly, reenvoicement can be achieved "through a dialogical system of intertextuality involving language, play and commercial exchange" (Kinder, 1991, p. 23).

As Duc Lan sought alternative and more exciting behavioral models than those he had experienced in his real life, he experimented with role-playing, selecting and discarding models that had been offered in the video games. He was able to pretend he was like someone he would rather be—a Ninja Turtle, Splinter, one of Shredder's henchmen, or whoever struck his whim. Identification and imitation were transient rather than permanent as roles were adopted and discarded like dressing up in Halloween costumes or wearing team caps. As Duc Lan enacted and reenvoiced these games, he became both excited and dramatic—first pointing an imaginary hand gun, then assuming a karate pose and whirling about to demonstrate his awesome ability to destroy hundreds of the enemy (armed foot soldiers) in what Kline (1993) called identity-transformation play.

An excerpt from my field notes combined with a tape transcript demonstrates Duc Lan's storytelling ability; as he talks he acts out much of the aggression in his martial arts' demonstrations and quick movements:

> Excitedly, Duc Lan told me that Saturday was his eighth birthday. "I buy one game. I won't tell you the name. It is a secret. You must guess it, Linda, you get only one chance to guess the name or you

lose." I make an offhand guess about the birthday game and give up. "Ninja Turtles Four," he announces, "A Super Nintendo game!" As Duc Lan detailed the playing of the game, I realized how self-assured he appeared to be as a speaker when he was enwrapped in this fantasy language. His customary stilted phrases gave way to fuller sentences and his discourse style was not unconnected as it was in conversation with the classroom teacher. Intensely describing every maneuver, it became evident when Duc Lan is the knower, the role like that of a teacher, he feels empowered. Perhaps, that is why he engages me in these detailed conversations as he knows I don't know about game playing. From his conversation, I could glean the general goals of the game. "It's a fighting game and really *violent* with lots of foot soldiers," he bellows. As he talks, he demonstrates the video moves with accompanying martial arts gestures. "The bad guy says, 'I am going to mangle you and blast you into smithereens.' I let him have it on his head and flatten him.. . . .The monster dies. POW!!" Knowing that violence is amplified, I ask him continually, "Duc Lan, is this a violent game?" He responds with "Nah! . . . it's fun." Dismissing my concern, he persists with the retelling of the game, delivering the dialogue in a bullying tone. I nod accordingly but begin to suspect that his definition of violent may be skewed. Continually, I keep trying to redirect the conversation to talking about his birthday party. It was a constant struggle as he was obsessed with the game description. Bits and pieces began to fit together. Just as I tried to piece the puzzle parts together, he interjected with the continuation of the new video game, "Wait! They're bonus stages!" I rebut by asking quizzically, "Did you have a birthday cake, Duc Lan?" "Yes, but I must tell you about the bonus stages . . .you will be amazed." I lost my turn to talk. Like a master storyteller telling a cliff-hanger, he continues on, "Wait, it's not over yet . . . You have to kill the master, Shredder, who is very **hard** to beat." My 60-minute tape has come to a halt. But he was not finished. "I rapped the game, I got a lot of points. 990 points!" Mastery of the game was of utmost importance.

Duc Lan's communicative style is distinguished by the fact that, in many of his conversations about video playing, the lines of dialogue were constructed like vivid lines in a drama. His emotional involvement with the game often made him forget his own experiences and social knowledge. Acting and talking like the characters, or identity-transformation play, he imagined the world from their perspective. In many ways, this was similar to action instead of meaning. One doesn't have to understand, just say the right words. The animation of his voice breathed life into imaginary but violent video characters and the plot of the game. Tannen (1987) calls this type of animated conversation "constructed dialogue," imagining a possible world to account for such events.

Joy is often sweetest in the sharing. By being a "someone" with whom he could share his video world (perhaps I was the only one), I provided a channel from the video world to reality. Without such a channel, the video experiences remained only in his head. Small wonder he didn't want to waste time with birthday cakes when, instead, I could offer him the opportunity to break the essentially isolating experience of reliving the playing of video games. Through sharing, he could bring his all-consuming passion into a social context—making the video world (and him) more real.

Video Scripts as Story

Bettelheim (1976) recommends exposing children to traditional tales that allow them to learn about human progress and possible solutions. In so doing, he believes children learn that struggling against adversity is unavoidable, but they can emerge victorious if they directly confront their difficulties. These traditional motifs present archetypical characters who are both good and evil and who are enmeshed in plots that ultimately lead to the truism that evil does not pay. Children empathize with just characters and their struggles and reject the bad knowing that eventually good will be triumphant. Similarly, video stories have a clear relationship with the narrative conventions and themes of traditional literature. In much the same way, the video games comprise archetypical characters such as Luigi and Mario and the Renaissance Turtles who are victorious in conquests against evil opponents. The games, with their simulated combat, martial arts themes and plots, primarily focus on adventure quests where the player struggles with a villain for a prize. But there is a difference. Unlike literature, here there is the tendency to resolve conflict through repeated aggression. The prototypes of video games are gendered texts—He-Man combats or heroic narratives, played in the underground labyrinths and loosely borrowed from legend and literature.

Gender bias and stereotyping is widespread and pervasive. Females are portrayed as minor characters who amplify certain values mainly as victims, as dependents, as sex objects, and not as initiators of actions. The emphasis is not on richly layered plot or characterization but on action-adventure quests, rescue motifs, damsels in distress, the visual display of violence and high-tech weaponry.

Provenzo (1991), explains the difference between literature and video game plots by pointing out that in video games the enemy remains anonymous, which diffuses responsibility for any actions: "There is no understanding of why things are the way they are—no history, no context, simply a threat and the need to act" (p. 126). Since video games depend upon dexterity rather than reason, they indiscriminately reward or punish both moral and immoral behavior. Thus, video plots must depend on force in game scenarios instead of moral reasoning to carry the action. While children's literature contains many moments of conflict, it is the characters who make moral decisions and contemplate the reasons for their decisions:

> In a literary story the author has time to develop the characters into fully rounded human beings. The reader knows the nature and pressures of each individual and can understand and empathizes with the character. If the tone of the author is one of compassion for the characters, if others in the story show concern or horror for a brutal act, the reader gains perspective (Huck, Hepler and Hickman, 1987, pp. 466–67).

Within the genre of action-adventure video games, plot and character take a back seat to action. The main emphasis is on the visual display of violence. The text revolves around spectacular fights, gun play, torture, and battles equipped with modern weaponry and endless magic powers. Nodelman (1990) questions whether video game players will develop a concept of narrative conventions. "Individual events don't build into a consistent or meaningful plot. Without a cohesive pattern, there is no suspense, and so the ending isn't climactic; it interrupts what has become the main pleasure, the continuing process of the game itself" (p. 47). If this is so, game playing might hinder a genuine understanding and appreciation of more conventional stories. What is the merit of a story compared to a video game? Story is a complex reality, a pattern of cause and effect underlying actions, while video games offer a simplistic controlled environment.

Unquestionably, the playing of video games involves children in more than viewing. This has implications for social behavior. Provenzo (1991) points out that video games are not neutral and are in fact encroaching on and redefining our culture. Unlike the flat two dimensional surfaces of a picture storybook, the enhanced graphics are compelling. What captures children's fascination is the visual dynamism. Video technology can defy the physical laws of the universe with repeating actions and dazzling objects that can jump, fly, spin, accelerate, whirl, disappear, reappear, transform shape, size, and color. This, of course, amplifies combative encounters often making them a detailed and bizarre spectacle.

Although a competent reader, Duc Lan chose not to read picture storybooks or borrow books from the school library. In this transcribed excerpt, his views about the lackluster nature of books are apparent:

Duc Lan: I don't like to read . . . it's no fun . . . it takes too much time. I just like reading game instructions because they're short.

Linda: I like reading and I have been borrowing lots of neat books from the library.

Duc Lan: I don't go. I just buy them. I have *Bambi* and *Snow White*. I got them at the supermarket . . . I read them already . . . I'm finished now.

Linda: I have lots of favorite books. I keep adding more to my list. I just added another favorite story which is about a trickster, *Iktomi and the Boulder* (Goble, 1988). Have you read it?

Duc Lan: Nah! My favorite one is the *Three Little Pigs*. I like the part where the wolf chases the pigs, except the wolf has no weapons. But the end is not very good.

Linda: I rather like the ending of that story. The wolf gets punished.

Duc Lan: Nothing happens in the end. The wolf falls in the pot and that's all that happens. He loses all his powers and doesn't come back. Just the end.

Unlike video games, for Duc Lan the chase game in *The Three Little Pigs* fizzled in the end. In a video game, there is no end—everyone comes back to life. Videos are loops, the player ends up back where he started, repeating the action. For Duc Lan, the picture book paled in comparison with the pulsating action and enhanced graphics of the video game. After all, there were no story characters rotating, accelerating, disappearing, changing into a hue of brilliant colors. A daily diet of dust-ups and punching out electronic bullies has limited the pleasure derived from reading experiences.

What is the message of video games? Unlike other forms of narratives, what happens in video games has no relation to the moral choices made by characters in books or the reasons for their decisions (Nodelman, 1990, p. 47). Because of this, there is an overwhelming sense of dehumanization, with unfeeling portrayals of victims of violence as worthless, subhuman, and expendable, hence justifying action against them. What may be alarming is that players soon learn that aggression is a method of conflict resolution. If someone is in the way, players are programmed to annihilate them before they get to you and you lose one of your diminishing powers! The message communicated by the games is that violence is not only accepted, it is necessary to win. Thus, the goals pursued are not connected to the larger culture.

Pretending: Stepping into the Shoes of Violent Heroes

"Pretend violence," which takes place in a context of clear humor or slapstick, or within the framework of a delineated fantasy, carries no greater impact than a Monty Python pratfall or a classical literature tumble such as that found in *Jack and the Beanstalk*. But video games are a whole new text, an immensely powerful agent that intersects between a child's culture and the culture of simulation. The games represent texts that can be interpreted on many social and cultural levels, conveying attitudes towards violence, technology, and gender. Video games place a heavy reliance on gendered action genres (the epic, romance quest, and western) in which males rise to heroism in the face of adversity. Games position players in ongoing serial combat where they must constantly fight off death and try to acquire new powers that will periodically grant them more lives. In part, then, these games are modeled on life extension—increasing the length of a turn or, in consumerist terms, getting more for your quarter (Kinder, 1991, p. 110).

Values are transmitted tacitly through the social relations and routines that characterize day-to-day school encounters (Giroux, 1985). It became clear in Duc Lan's classroom that the wide scope of video games impacted on children's attitudes, behaviors, views of the world, and cognitive abilities. It was apparent that how children interpret videos was not predicated on simple mimicry, but was mediated by the processes of social learning and identification, especially by stepping into the lives of aggressive characters. Simulating confrontations and mock battles with accompanying narrative dialogue, it was not unusual for video game players such as Duc Lan or others to engage in "combat play" when spaces opened within the daily classroom routines—conflict at the coat hooks, juggling for positions in class lineups, sharing circles, or sitting in literary discussions. Such dialogues illuminated the metaphors and images acquired from the games. "I got here first in line. Move back, dude, or I'll stab you." or "That's my eraser, Shellbrain. Give it back or I will decimate you with my Katana blade!" are reenvoiced beyond the earshot of the teacher, whom Duc Lan calls "The boss!" Most classroom turf problems were settled through threats—simulated fists and kicks. Similarly, Duc Lan chronicled these dazzling exploits in his writing when given the opportunity to make choices about what and how he wanted to express his ideas, feelings, or thoughts. This adulation of video characters and serialized narratives raises a concern that children may believe in the appropriateness of violence as a ready solution to interpersonal problems.

Although Duc Lan's behavior was simulating aggression and negativism, he did not get into actual fights but relished observing playground skirmishes on the sidelines. He commented about who got "mangled, decimated or blasted to smithereens." His interpersonal relationships were detached from any particular group. Most of the other boys in the class were soccer or hockey enthusiasts watching weekly matches on the television, comparing scores, and glorifying physical encounters. Duc Lan was not interested in sports. His favorite games were Nintendo or Game Boy because in his words, "I like all the shooting and fighting." Part of the appeal was Duc Lan's identification with the strongest and toughest video characters, sharing with them the feeling of power and heroism. He ignored the storyline and claimed he did not care who was the good guy or who was the bad guy. He just cared who won and that was the one he liked. Focusing on the fight scenes he switched his allegiance to whomever was winning—Leonardo, Krang, or even Baxter.

Winning fostered Duc Lan's intense competitive spirit. This attitude was transferred into most of his school tasks including spelling a word correctly, doing math, getting a story sequence right, or filling the most pages in his daily writing journal. Underscored was also a sense of honoring the family by doing well at school. Whether competition was idiosyncratic, cultural, or due to video game manipulation, he tried to outwit, outperform, and beat everyone in the class. Although Duc Lan thinks his actions are appropriate and expected, his sense of individualism is evident in the following interaction as he separates himself from a peer.

> Minh Tan turns to Duc Lan sitting beside him: "How do you spell friends?" he asks nicely.
>
> "Spell your own words, Minh Tan," says Duc Lan.
>
> "I won't ask you anything the rest of the day if you will just spell my word," begs Minh Tan.
>
> Duc Lan nods and spells the word rapidly, too rapidly for his classmate to hear all the letters, "F R E N Z"
>
> "Could you say it again, Duc Lan? You were too fast," pleaded Minh Tan.
>
> "Too bad, you lost your chance. I am the winner, say your prayers, slimeball," was Duc Lan's reply.

Bowers (1980) may offer some possible understanding of what underlies Duc Lan's actions. He maintains that despite an emphasis

on the sense of community within our culture, "individualism remains a dominant cultural model in our society," both economically
and socially (p. 13). Bowers identifies the operant principle underlying the organization and structure of the majority of games as individualism. He claims "the emphasis on violence and aggression found
in the games is crucial to maintaining the model of the individual as
an autonomous and self-directed being" (p. 13). Turkle (1984) supports this idea by arguing that what is being pursued in the video
game is not just a score or a win but an altered state, "a second self"
(p. 71). I eventually came to learn that Duc Lan wasn't just participating in the role of one of the video characters; he had programmed
himself to act like them. Throughout the classroom learning activities, an oppositional climate permeated: me (Duc Lan) vs. them.

Reenvoicement

Throughout the school year, Duc Lan remained ambivalent towards his classmates. Both the fantasies and video games he related
to tended to highlight the hostile and competitive aspects of interpersonal relationships, in contrast to his limited capacity for trust-
ing relationships with peers. Underlying his ambivalence was the
confounding question: if real guns and weaponry were available to
him, would he be assaultive? That remains an enigma. He seemed
desensitized to violence. Fists, elbows, and knees were always available. What about sticks, stones, and other implements? Violent as-
saults were not uncommon in neighboring schools. Somewhere
between the hopefully unavailable gun and the available elbow,
guidelines need to be drawn with respect to replicable violent portrayals involving techniques and instruments available to children
predisposed to initiate such acts.

Does video violence engender aggressive behavior? Research is
not conclusive. However, there appears to be a feedback loop between
watching violent games and being aggressive. According to Huesmann (1986), exposure to violence does appear to increase aggression,
but being aggressive also seems to increase preferences for violent
games. Perhaps because aggressive behavior leads to peer rejection,

aggressive children may have fewer options for alternative activities. Thus, video game playing might occupy that space for Duc Lan.

Envoicing the violence garnered from video games often surfaced in Duc Lan's journal entries. His persistent use of video language appeared to be a deliberate attempt to mark his social identity and to communicate with his personal voice whether "school appropriate" or not:

> *Yesterday I played a game called Tiddly Winks with Phillip. We need a cup and coins. All we half to do is to throw the coins in the cup. If I got it in the cup, I got to go again. If I don't get in the cup then the other person's turn. I won. I got all the turns. I killed the slime ball enemy.*

Admonished by the teacher, the last sentence was erased without critical dialogue about its persistent recurrence. But what is Duc Lan telling his teacher? It opens some questions about writing conversations. Do we deal with the problem of video game content by excluding them from classroom conversations or do we engage in dialogue? Do we teach children to question the prevailing social practices of the video games in a sustained critical manner or do we preserve the hegemony of the consumer market—video violence happens outside of school life? How about a reality check on video stories? Fairy tales are potent because they do say something about real life, although perhaps in fantastical ways. Do video tales say something about reality, too?

Video topics are prepackaged. Since the electronic games supply teammates and opponents, all youngsters have to do is push the buttons for instant role models who are engaged in serial combat and scripted language. All the while the games are permeated with an overarching mood of violence and destruction—a contagion spreading into classroom writing communities. Many children like Duc Lan feel close to the video characters, have a strong sense of their reality, and feel akin to them in spirit as between real friends. When queried about what makes a friend Duc Lan said:

> Leonardo is my best and only friend because I like the way his stick punches his enemy and kills them better than any one else. That's why I want to write about his adventures. I think about him all the time. We are buddies.

Kinder (1991) believes that as a domesticated media, video games may be replacing the family as the "collective mind" or the "primary cybernetic system of feedback loops" (p. 23). Similarly, Kline (1993) cautions about market goods that substitute for and "displace" the traditional patterns of family relations:

> Something is missing from childhood, . . . when we give a child a musical tape of children's songs because we don't have time to sing to or with them; . . . when we let them watch fantasies on TV, without reading to them or exposing them to the intimacy of personal storytelling; when we give a child Nintendo, but fail to teach them the finger games or craft skills (knitting, carpentry, gardening) that have been traditions within our families (p. 13).

Changing the Circumstances

The impact of video game playing on various facets of social behavior is a critical but increasingly complex question. The relationship between participation in violent games and subsequent aggressive behavior appears to be not clearly causal. Issues of realism, strength of identification, family attitudes and behavior, habituation and desensitization, gender differences, the amount and purpose of game playing, all interact to determine whether an individual will actually behave aggressively after participating in video games. As educators, what position do we take? There are no easy answers. It is not reasonable to expect children to develop the ability to play, talk and write richly and expansively if their models demonstrate dominance, submission, hatred, contempt, and callousness. They need to have models of caring and commitment, joy and zest for life if they are to express these themes in their play and their talk. We must open critical dialogue about video games; ignoring their existence will not diminish their social implications.

What were the effects of game playing on Duc Lan's self-image, relationships, and social skills? Video games may be effective in suggestion of techniques but may not actually cause aggravation of antisocial behavior. It may not cause Duc Lan to be a bully, but it can alert him to new techniques of bullying. The potential role of video games may be a stimulus of real-life violence.

Entertainment of children requires supervision. Supervising children is basically a parental responsibility; parents determine what type of toys their children play with, and how much. They also can interpret what is happening on the screen. They act as models, gatekeepers, and interpreters for the media. However, the extent to which they serve this function is in question. Where parental supervision is inadequate, then there is a responsibility to be shared between game creators and the school. This needs to be addressed in a more open forum.

Present theories may be inadequate to explain what is happening to children in today's society. That is why teachers are at a loss when deciding how to handle the recasting of violent video play. We may be past the point where our actions to restrain violence can be confined to the classroom. It may be time to speak out against the forces that are changing our children into violence-focused players. We need to further explore whether such play is a distortion of a healthy childhood and rethink what living in such a violent society is doing to our children's learning and play.

Note

1. An earlier version of this chapter was presented to the Canadian Association for the Study of Women and Education as part of the Canadian Society for the Study of Education Conference in Calgary, Alberta, Canada, June 1994.

References

Bakhtin, M. (1981). *The dialogical imagination*. Austin, TX: University of Texas Press.

Bettelheim, B. (1976). *The uses of enchantment: The meaning and importance of fairy tales*. New York: Knopf.

Bettelheim, B. (1987, March). The importance of play. *The Atlantic Monthly*, pp. 35–46.

Bowers, C. A. (1980). *The cultural dimensions of educational computing: Understanding the non-neutrality of technology*. New York: Teachers College.

Calkins, L. (1986). *The art of teaching writing*. Portsmouth, NH: Heinemann.

Fuller, M. (1984). Dimensions of gender in school: Reinventing the wheel? In R. G. Burgess (Ed.), *The research process in educational settings: Ten case studies*. Lewes, UK: Falmer Press.

Giroux, H. A. (1983). *Theory and resistance in education. A pedagogy for the oppressed*. New York: Begin and Garvey.

Giroux, H. A. (1985, May). Teachers as transformative intellectuals. *Social Education* 49, (5), 376–79.

Goble, P. (1988). Iktomi and the boulder: A plains Indian story. Danbury, CT: Orchard Books.

Gronland, G. (1992). Coping with Ninja Turtle play in my kindergarten classroom. *Young Children, 48* (1), 21–25.

Hicks, D. (1992). Ninja Turtles and other super heroes: A case study of one literacy learner. *Linguistics and Education, 4* (1), 59–105.

Hubbard, R. (1989). *Authors of pictures, draughtsmen of words*. Portsmouth, NH: Heinemann.

Huck, C., Hepler, S., and Hickman, J. (1987). *Children's literature in the elementary school*. New York: Holt, Rinehart & Winston.

Huesmann, L. R. (1986). Psychological processes promoting the relation between exposure to media violence and aggressive behavior by the viewer. *Journal of Social Issues, 42*, 125–39.

Huesmann, L. R. (1994). Aggressive behavior: Current perspectives. NY, NY: Plenum Press.

Kinder, M. (1991). *Playing with power in movies, television, and video games: Muppet babies to Teenage Mutant Ninja Turtles*. Berkeley: University of California Press.

Kline, S. (1993). Out of the garden: Toys and children's culture in the age of TV marketing. Culture and Communication Series. Toronto: Garamond Press.

Mies, M. (1991). Women's research or feminist research? The debate surrounding feminist science and methodology. In Fonow, M. M. and A. Cook (Eds.), *Beyond methodology.* Indianapolis, IND: Indiana University Press.

Neilsen, L. (1989). *Literacy and living.* Portsmouth, NH: Heinemann Educational Books.

Nodelman, P. (1990). *The pleasures of children's literature.* New York, Longman.

Protherough, R. (1983). *Encouraging writing.* London: Methuen.

Provenzo, E. F. (1991). *Video kids. Making sense of Nintendo.* Cambridge: Harvard University Press.

Soper, W. B. (1993). Junk-time junkies: An emerging addiction among students. *School Counselor, 31* (1), 40–43.

Spindler, G. and Spindler, L. (Eds.). (1987). *Interpretative ethnography of education: At home and abroad.* Hillsdale, NJ: Lawrence Erlbaum.

Tamivarra, J. and Enright, D. S. (1986). On eliciting information: Dialogues with child informants. *Anthropology & Education Quarterly, 17,* 218–38.

Tannen, D. (1987). *You just don't understand. Women and men in conversation.* New York: Ballantine Books.

Tannen, D. (1987). The orality of literature and the literacy of conversation. In Langer, J. (Ed.), *Language, literacy and culture: Issues of society and schooling* (pp. 67–88). Norwood, NJ: Ablex Publishing Co.

Turkle, S. (1984). *The second self: computers and the human spirit.* New York: Simon & Schuster.

Walker, H. M., Colvin, G. and Ramsay, E. (1994) *Antisocial behavior in school: Strategies and best practices.* Toronto: Brooks/Cole Publishing.

Watson-Gegeo, K. (1988). Ethnography in ESL: Defining the essentials. *TESOL Quarterly, 22,* 575–92.

Chapter 6

Discourses and Silencing in Classroom Space[1]

Mutindi Ndunda

This chapter is a personal narrative, an account of the experiences that have been my reality as a black woman, a mother, and an international student in Canada. These experiences are shaped by race and gender factors with historical, social, cultural, economic, and political dimensions that create hierarchies among humanity. These experiences are not unique to me. I questioned the importance of writing this narrative. Part of me wished to remain silent as it was safer. The other part wished to speak, as a way of coming to terms with the meanings and implications of these experiences to myself, to my children, and to others.

After much agonizing, I took the risk of breaking my silence to speak about my experiences. Speaking creates the possibility for change in the course of our lives and history. As my ethnic people say, an idea in your head is useful only when it is spoken. In this chapter, I examine experiences which reinforced my alienation and feelings of otherness. The aim is not only to highlight the Eurocentricity of educational systems in the North and their demands on the "other," but also to make change a possibility as we discuss these issues with honesty and sincerity for the benefit of all the stakeholders: educators, children, parents, community.

Becoming Conscious of Me

In the summer of 1988, I left my country, two children, and a husband, to undertake graduate studies in Canada. Exciting and prestigious as it was to win a scholarship, my early experiences in Canada were rather daunting. I began to have a deep realization of my difference or otherness. I began to have a new realization of my belonging to the black race. I attempted to analyze the nature of the differences I represented (or the differences represented in me) and their relationship to the silencing, devaluation, and sense of worthlessness that I felt. I became obsessed and terrified by my "otherness." My accent began to sound very strange, almost unbearable, and inherently inferior to those of other graduate students who did not have to make extra efforts to be understood. I felt the need to remain silent, to save myself the agony of being told over and over that I could not be understood: communication seemed a never ending "pardon me."

I felt silenced and I silenced myself. I withdrew from classroom discussions. I refrained from participation except when I was specifically asked. Such moments were terrifying; I was overwhelmed with fear as I sought ways to construct a coherent response. I felt like a stranger and an alien. Although, by definition, I was a visible minority, I became and preferred to be invisible, even though opting to remain silent and invisible meant that I would not get marks for class participation.

The struggle that I engaged in went unnoticed. At least, it never became obvious that my professors or my colleagues were aware of my struggles. I did not perceive any attempts to create an environment that addressed my fears. I longed to talk to a Canadian in a safer place about my experiences—maybe in the corridors or in the washrooms—somewhere. I wished that somebody would give me time to answer the casual North American "how are you's" that were asked of me. Nobody took the time to understand my feelings of alienation.

Becoming Conscious of Race

Throughout history, African/black people have been placed at the bottom of the racial hierarchies that were created in order to dehumanize them and justify atrocities such as slavery, colonialism, neocolonialism, and apartheid. As I began to understand that my experiences were structured by race and power issues, I felt paralyzed at the thought of dealing with racism—an unnecessary complication in my complex life. My confidence went "down the tube." My dream of a career and the possibility of breaking the poverty cycle that delineates the lives of most of my female counterparts in the South began to evaporate. My dream to achieve goals that my mother and many women of her generation were denied and the vision that gave me the strength to leave two little children in Africa were challenged. The hope of a better future for my children had helped me reconcile the contradictions of the assumed gender roles of an African woman as first a mother and a wife and the desire/passion to pursue a career far away from home.

I did not attempt to bring my experiences into class discourse: they were not welcome in this space. In group discussions, my contributions were either not understood or not acknowledged by group members. I felt dumb. I began to believe the words of a former Canadian High Commissioner to one African country who said that "Africa has nothing to offer." I shared Williams's 1905 lament:

> The colored girl [woman] . . . is not known and hence not believed in; she belongs to a race that is best designated by the term problem, and she lives beneath the shadow of that problem which envelops and obscures her (cited in Collins, 1991, p. 5).

At this point of despair, the words of my mother and brother echoed in the distance: Hardships and trials don't last forever; endured, they bring out the gold in you. My brother's motto was: "I will never sink under the load of despair."

I needed to do what I had to do to complete my program and return home where the politics of the skin color did not structure my daily life. I could not go back empty-handed. Nobody would understand the issues that contributed to my failure. I was determined to do the best that I could within the constraints of my situation and to achieve my goal without challenging or contesting the circumstances that structured my experiences. I became aware of the conditions that force the "other" to put their energies into crafting racism-survival techniques rather than in developing themselves and their new communities.

Although I felt that I did not have the skills to cope with racism, my perseverance in growing up in a rural village where I had to struggle to get the basics of living helped me put together a scheme of survival. Had I not crafted some survival techniques, I would certainly have joined the multitude of students who have been flushed out of the education system under the label failure.

I survived the first year of graduate school, and went to my home country to do my field work. Funding from my sponsor allowed me to go back to see my young children whom I had not seen for almost a year. I knew I could not leave my children behind again. I had to struggle and raise their airfares to bring them back with me. Having my family with me, though physically and materially challenging, gave me the strength to handle the constraints that I experienced as the "other." However, I had to help my children understand their experiences as black children in a predominantly white society.

My children attended a day care and kindergarten and later an elementary school in which they were the only black children. They were not exempted from racist experiences in the classrooms and in the playgrounds. My children's experiences worried me most because they were young and had not had a chance to develop their confidence in an environment where skin color was not a criterion. They had not had the opportunity to learn in environments where as bell hooks (1994) observes, teachers knew your family and teaching was seen as an act of freedom. They had not been in environments where their experiences as black children were recognized as central and significant. I was concerned about my children growing up in an environment where black people have tended to be seen as social deviants with inadequacies that have to be remedied (Solomos, 1988).

Becoming Conscious of Feminist Politics

After completing my master's degree, I got the opportunity to undertake a Ph.D. program. My family and my professors encouraged me to pursue the program despite lack of funding. For my Ph.D., I moved from my science background to explore gender issues in education. I opted for courses that seemed to offer the possibility of engaging in the interrogation of the pedagogical process. I looked for the space where we could think seriously about pedagogy in relation to the practice of freedom (hooks, 1994, p. 6).

However, this was not to be the case. In this space, silencing of the "other" took two forms: the choice of texts and their producers, and the discourses that implied homogeneity of students' experiences. Teaching approaches that do not value the experiences of all students do not provide the space for critical thinking and the interrogation of our lived experiences. The negative impact of such approaches on black children and youth is well documented and has resulted in high dropout rates among black students in North America and in Britain.

Exclusion

Women's studies is the main educational representation of feminism (Watt and Cook, 1990). The courses attempt to explore the experiences of women and their contributions in the public and private spheres in the past and present (Abir-Am and Outram, 1987). Attempts are made to show the constraints that women faced and continue to face as participants in the production of knowledge. But participating in these programs is problematic. Most women's studies courses reflect the experiences of white women, assuming that the category of Woman is universal. There is minimal effort to include materials that reflect experiences of other women, particularly women from the South and Aboriginal women. To deny different voices entry into the discourses of women's experiences is a power issue.

Women in the North, like their male counterparts, are more privileged than their Southern and Aboriginal counterparts. They have access to the resources (education, the right discourse, time, and money) required to produce knowledge. It is not surprising that feminist studies about African women continue to be written and produced mainly by non-African scholars based outside the continent (Mbilinyi, 1991). Most Southern women have to put in over fifteen hours of work per day to put bread on the table. The debt crisis and the structural adjustment policies designed to ensure that Southern countries meet their debt repayments to the Northern countries have caused untold suffering to women and their dependents in the South.

Some Western feminists have tried to analyze critically conditions of women in the South, but most have continued to perpetuate the image of a monolithic, third-world woman oppressed by a singular monolithic patriarchy (Mohanty, 1991). These images deny third-world women their diversity of experiences and agency in the midst of social, economic, and political crises that delineate their lives. Universalizing women's experiences silences and negates the experiences of those who are excluded. The excluded women, who tend to be a minority in graduate classes, often comply with the status quo in order to survive and to avoid the repercussions that might follow their contestations.

The assumption that women's experiences are universal reinforces stereotypes about those women who do not fit into these mainstream discourses—working-class women, and women from the South. Views such as the universal oppression of women by men, the home as a site of oppression of women, the strategies through which women may become liberated, and the attributes of those liberated women, are particularly disturbing.

Colonialization

The explanations given for the present conditions of women do not address crucial historical, colonial, and neocolonial policies that exacerbate gender inequalities in countries in the South. The predominant Western feminist view of liberation constructs traditional cultures as oppressive, thus taking the same positions as the imperialists. The feminist notion of what a liberated woman should be is antagonizing.

The use of the Western norm as the referent point on meanings of liberation, splits people in the South into two groups—the
oppressors (men) and the oppressed (women). This dichotomy obscures the complexity of female-male and female-female relationships within any society. It also denies the power women held in
precapitalist settings and absolves the colonialists of their contribution to the abject poverty that delineates most Southerners'
lives.

Oppression and liberation might have different meanings to
different women—meanings that we can only begin to appreciate if
our classrooms become spaces of intervention. Our classrooms
need to be spaces where we can interrogate texts such as newspaper
articles which portray women in Islamic countries as oppressed by
their traditional Islamic society (The Women of the Veil, 1992).
Often, non-Western traditions are portrayed as barriers to women's
participation in education and the public sphere. This Eurocentric
perception of "other" creates a polarity between traditions and
modernization whereby some women are modern or liberated and
other women are oppressed and in need of liberation. When these
attitudes are propagated by feminists in their writing, in the media,
and in the classroom, it becomes difficult for a woman, like me, to
speak of my experiences and knowledge of traditional lives which
would contradict the powerful written/published word.

While there might be limited resources available on other
women/people in Western libraries, it would be possible to address their absence by making our classrooms spaces where edu-
cators/teachers and students can raise critical questions and
interrogate texts as cultural texts in the light of our experiences.
This would make the classroom a less harmonious space than
many educators would want it to be. The desire for harmony in
our classrooms does not address the real meaning of cultural diversity. As bell hooks (1994) observes, the idea of a harmonious
classroom is a colonizing fantasy.

Our vision of teaching, and our practices, must change to reflect the reality of our diverse classrooms for the sake of our children. Therefore, classrooms (in academia, high schools, elementary
schools, and kindergartens) need to become spaces where students'
experiences are valued. Classes need to become spaces where
"other" women or people are not only objects of discussions, but

where women and men of different cultural, social, economic, and political backgrounds feel safe, to share their experiences. In addition, there is need for courage and honesty in our struggle to address inequities along race, gender, and class lines.

For white women to explore how their color privileges them requires honesty and risk taking. Privileged women must be prepared to challenge the structures that perpetuate and reinforce their privilege if those of us who are at the periphery are to take them seriously. Presently, it appears as though feminists skate around the issue of white as a color and how it privileges them. They tend to exclude discourses that might rock their comfort zones. Under the universal banner of women's experiences, women like me are coerced to assume the stance that men are our oppressors while I know well enough that our sisterhood is not based on equal grounds. bell hooks (1984) made the same observation:

> White women who dominate feminist discourse today rarely question whether or not their perspective on women's reality is true to the lived experiences of women as a collective group. Nor are they aware of the extent to which their perspectives reflect race and class biases. . . . Racism abounds in the writings of white feminists, reinforcing white supremacy and negating the possibility that women will bond politically across ethnic and racial boundaries (p. 3).

hooks (1994) continues to point out that white feminists, who are busy publishing papers and books on eradicating racism, still remain patronizing and condescending when they relate to black women. She notes that they make us the objects of their privileged discourse on race, and as objects we remain unequal inferiors (p. 12). Mohanty (1991) also addresses the encumbrance of Western feminists' scholarship in its construction of a monolithic third-world woman through appropriation and codification of scholarship and knowledge. This scholarship/text, Mohanty argues, is a directly political and discursive practice in that it is purposeful and ideological (p. 53).

Discourse of Western scholarship has political effects and implications beyond the immediate feminist or disciplinary audience (Mohanty, 1991). It impacts on women's lives in the South through the foreign policies followed by Northern governments. It comes from those schools whose graduates are hired by their governments as development agents and who are taken as authorities to define the lives of women in developing countries. Stamp (1995) argues that the facile but compelling popular imagery of an African woman that reduces her to the anguished, helpless mother holding a famished child has influenced policies initiated and supported by international organizations. These women's capacity to act is countered by the perceptions of them as pawns of men.

Gender

The perception that all women are pawns of men is derived from the argument of the universal oppression of women by men which requires universal liberatory practices for women to rid themselves of the yoke of oppression. Liberating practices that call for sexual separatism advocated by some feminists as the ultimate goal of the feminist movement can only work in the social, cultural, economic, and political contexts within which they are theorized. This reactionary separatism is rooted in the conviction that male supremacy is an absolute aspect of our culture, that women have only two alternatives: accept it or withdraw from it to create subcultures (Segal, 1987; hooks, 1984; Jaggar, 1983).

hooks (1984) notes that since the inception of the feminist movement, men have never been called upon to assume responsibility for actively struggling to end sexist oppression. Men, they argued, were all-powerful misogynist oppressors—the enemy. Women were the oppressed victims (p. 67). hooks argues that the insistence on a "women only" feminist movement and a virulent antimale stance reflects the race and class background of the participants.

Antimale sentiments alienate many poor and working-class women from the movement. Life experiences of these women show that they have much more in common with men of their race and/or class. They have had the experience of struggling with them. In Africa, women have fought for their countries' independence alongside their men. Poor women in Latin America, Asia, and Africa continue the struggle to end class oppression alongside their male counterparts (Davies, 1987). In the United States, black women have contributed equally to the antiracist struggle. hooks (1984) notes that there is a special tie binding people who struggle collectively for liberation. This does not deny the gender inequities that exist in these communities, which must also be addressed, but for most women from the South, the separatist solution is not a viable option. Women who are socially, economically, and politically independent of their spouses or partners might see separation as an alternative. However, for most women in the South, particularly the rural poor, separatism is not a possibility even when desired.

Damian (1987) notes that women's submission to their partners in a sexual relationship is based not only on the machismo of men, but also on a certain material and social need to guarantee the relationship (p. 40). Colonialism exacerbated gender inequities in precapitalist societies by introducing laws and policies that favored men over women by making women dependents of men for economic resources. For instance, with the introduction of the land registration policy by the colonialist, land ownership was shifted from the family to individual men, limiting women's access to it. Education and other wage-earning opportunities were offered by the colonialist along gender and racial lines. Most women have access to land and education only through spouses or male relatives. Over 80 percent of the rural population in Africa is women. These are women who have little or no education and who often have no source of income.

Community

Also related to the issue of men as oppressors and women as victims is the issue of reproductive labor, where women are deemed biologically responsible for child bearing and rearing. In the African context, the family, and in particular motherhood, offers a woman the opportunity for influence as both elder sister and mother of grown sons living in the same household. This implies that the concept of a family in the African context is complex. It is not a bounded unit of society that consists of a man and his family (Stamp, 1989).

McAdoo and Were (1987) conclude that, despite urbanization and the influence of Westernization, motherhood is still highly valued by most women in Africa because of what it symbolizes. Mbiti (1990) notes that among certain ethnic groups in Africa, the birth of a child symbolizes the birth of a community. In Kenya, for example, motherhood is a powerful conceptual weapon used by both progressive and conservative forces in the battle to define women's political and social place (Stamp, 1995). The perception that women are oppressed as mothers contradicts the women's belief in the importance of their role as mothers.

African-Americans have a different meaning for the homeplace. They have regarded the homeplace as a place of resistance. Without the homeplace, black women's consciousness and resistance to the dynamics of racism that stripped her of dignity and personal power would have been impossible. bell hooks (1990) points out that throughout history, African-Americans have recognized the subversive value of homeplace, of having access to private space where we do not directly encounter white racist aggression (p. 47). hooks perceives the denial of oppressed people to make a homeplace as an attempt by whites to subjugate black people and as an attempt to deny women a political site for the creation of female identity and political consciousness:

> An effective means of white subjugation of black people globally has been the perpetual construction of economic and social structures that deprive many folks of the means to make homeplace. . . . It is no accident that the South African apartheid regime systematically attacks and destroys black efforts to construct homeplace, however tenuous, that small private reality where black women and men can renew their spirits and recover themselves. It is no accident that this homeplace, as fragile and as transitional as it may be, a makeshift shed, a small bit of earth where one rests, is always subject to violation and destruction. For when people no longer have the space to construct homeplace, we cannot build a meaningful community of resistance (hooks, 1990, pp. 46–47).

My experiences as a black woman and an international student have made me understand the importance of a homespace or the space that I regard as a home away from home. To me it is a relatively safe space where I feel valued despite negative experiences that characterize my daily life. In this space we share our pain, frustrations, and successes. It is the space where I take inventory of my experiences and find the strength to fight yet another day. This, however, does not deny the contradictions that I face in this home-place as I attempt to negotiate my responsibilities as an African woman, a mother, and a graduate student.

From a Site of Silence to a Site of Intervention

One of the unfortunate consequences of the exclusionary nature of most educational programs in the North, is that there are few ed-ucators who are ready to cope with the cultural diversity represented in present classroom settings. This makes challenging and contest-ing exclusions a risky undertaking. bell hooks (1984) notes the anger and hostility that was directed toward her when she pointed out that a reading list for a feminist theory course she had enrolled in had writings by white women and men and one black man, but had no material by or about blacks, Native American Indians, Hispanic, or Asian people. Not many students, particularly those from the South, have the courage to contest course materials presented to us in grad-uate programs. The environment to raise these issues without con-testing and challenging the powers that be is not available.

Attempts to criticize Eurocentrism seem futile given the na-ture of the problem and the power relations that determine stu-dent, professor, and institutional relationships. Unfortunately, our children's classrooms are delineated by even more powerful power relations of authority based on age, race, and gender among others. It is thus unimaginable for children to object to their exclusion in classrooms; rather it is more likely for them to begin to deny their culture, ethnicity, and heritage. Children can only be spared the agony of self-denial and erasure if our classrooms, at all levels, can become intervention sites.

There are risks in attempting to make classrooms interven-tion sites, particularly if you are a student. Conflicts of power and identification became real to me in a graduate class when I felt morally obliged to point out that I had been structured as an ob-ject in a research text that was presented as though it was neutral to a neutral audience. The text was two videos. The first showed acts of benevolence toward poor, homeless people. The helpers were all white and the homeless were black people. As I sat in that class and watched the process of feeding the homeless on a cold winter day, I felt myself located within the discourse of the narrative. I hoped that we would address the issue of homelessness as a social problem with political, historical, and economic underpinnings. I hoped that we would explore the issue of structural poverty as it pertains to the African-American people and to many other people of the world. To my surprise, frustration, and anger, these issues where not addressed.

The second video featured, coincidentally, a black girl from a stereotypical single-mother on welfare family and a white boy from a relatively "normal" family. Rather than address the issues suggested by these texts, I was asked what I thought of the videos. Why I was asked this question, I will never know. I felt like walking out. I hoped that my response (which was quite emotional) would offer the opportunity to problematise the images we had seen. What concerned me most about the images was that they could be used to reinforce stereotypes about African-American people and poverty in general, through lack of a critical analysis of the historical, social, economic, and political dimensions of the underlying conditions. This piece of ethnography did not in any way challenge widely held stereotypes about black people in relation to paid work, or stereotypes suggesting that Hispanics are lazy and that blacks prefer to sell drugs rather than work in a factory (Smith et al.; 1988). It did not provide the space to question the racist assumptions that blacks are genetically inferior, never as capable as their white peers, or even unable to learn (hooks, 1994).

My attempts to make the class a site of intervention and of critical analysis did not materialize for it meant introducing the subject of racism, a subject which would create disorder/disharmony. Silence was the weapon that was used against me. I had hoped that we, as educators and would-be researchers, would address these images and what they meant. More importantly, I had hoped we would begin to address the social, economic, and political conditions that structure peoples' lives and dichotomize them into Haves and Have Nots. This was an opportunity for us all to begin to address our own privileged positions and the social, economic, and political factors that maintain them. Nevertheless, this piece of work turned out to be yet another ethnography of horror, not of possibility! The silence was particularly unnerving. A week later, one of the white students told me that I should be grateful that I was allowed to voice my views!

The video intensified the pain and agony of my experiences with my children. I was concerned about my children who were subjected to similar materials and who had no mechanism for refusing these inferior racial positions. My children have been here for five years and they have continuously asked why they are black. They have been comparing who amongst them is fairer! I must note that it is not with a sense of pride that they ask me about the color of their skin. What are our responsibilities as teachers? Shouldn't we as educators learn to be sensitive to the impact of the material we choose to use or to exclude from our classrooms? Are we to continue the banking system of education, or should we help our students become critical thinkers by making our classrooms spaces where students can raise critical questions about pedagogical processes (hooks, 1994)?

There is a need to foster critical analyses of books and media productions, to tease out issues of inequalities along race, gender, and class categories. As bell hooks (1984) observes, the classroom setting is a crucial site for critical intervention. If the classroom does not become a site for critical intervention, then the field will be left to those thinkers who are primarily concerned with professional advancement and this would be a grave mistake (hooks, 1984).

When one takes the courage to intervene, it is important to distinguish between hostile criticism and criticism that is illuminating and enriches understanding. Criticism should be considered a way of offering insight without serving as a barrier to appreciation. If not, the prescription of colonialism and domination through our sharing of knowledge is reinforced:

> When we fail to make our classrooms sites of intervention and learning the process of liberation, we continue the unleashing of the cultural bomb to the oppressed to break their defiance against imperialism (WaThiong, 1984, p. 3).

We continue to annihilate a people's belief in their capacities and ultimately in themselves.

bell hooks (1994) notes the importance of educators abandoning their view of the contemporary classroom as a place of tranquillity and stability, arguing that it should be a risky place where teachers and students struggle to understand their everyday lives. She calls for teachers to renew their minds in order to transform educational institutions and society so that the way we live, teach, and work can reflect our joy in cultural diversity, our passion for justice, and our love of freedom (p. 34). This lends itself to the possibility of challenging conditions that continue to reinforce systemic violence that not only prevents certain groups of students from learning, but forces them to unlearn and reject knowledge about themselves as a people.

Note

1. An earlier version of this chapter was presented to the Canadian Association for the Study of Women and Education as part of the Canadian Society for the Study of Education Conference in Calgary, Alberta, Canada, June 1994.

References

Abir-Am, P. G., and Outram, D. (Eds.). (1987). *Uneasy careers and intimate lives.* New Brunswick, NJ: Rutgers University Press.

Colllins, P. H.. (1991). *Black feminist thought: Knowledge, consciousness, and the politics of empowerment.* New York: Routledge.

Davies, M. (Ed.). (1987). *Third world second sex.* Vol. 2. London: Zed Books.

Damian, E. G. (1987). Feminism and social struggle in Mexico. In M. Davies (Ed.), *Third world second sex.* Vol. 2. London: Zed Books.

hooks, b. (1984). *Feminist theory from margin to center.* Boston: South End.

hooks, b. (1990). *Yearning: Race, gender, and cultural politics.* Boston: South End.

hooks, b. (1994). *Teaching to transgress: Education as the practice of freedom.* New York: Routledge.

Jaggar, M. A. (1983). *Feminist politics and human nature.* Totowa, NJ: Rowman & Littlefield.

Mbilinyi, M. (1991). Reports from four women's groups in Africa. *Signs, 16,* (4), 846–69.

Mbiti, J. S. (1990). *African Religions and Philosophy (2nd edition)* Chicago, IL. Heinemann Educational Publishers.

McAdoo, P. H. and Were, M. (1987). Extended family involvement and roles of urban Kenyan women. In R. Terborg-Penn, S. Harley, and A. Rushing (Eds.), *Women in Africa and the African diaspora.* Washington, DC: Howard University.

Mohanty, C. T. (1991). Under western eyes: Feminist scholarship and colonial discourse. In C. T. Mohanty, A. Russo, and L. Torres (Eds.), *Third world women and the politics of feminism.* Indianapolis, IN: Indiana University .

Segal, L. (1987). *Is the future female? Troubled thoughts on contemporary feminism.* London: Virago.

Smith, J., Collins, J., Hopkins, K. T. and Muhammand, A. (Eds.). (1988). *Racism, sexism and the world-system.* Westport, CT: Greenwood Press.

Solomos, J. (1988). Institutionalised racism: Policies of marginalization in education and training. In P. Cohen and H. S. Bains (Eds.), *Multiracist Britain.* Hampshire: Macmillan Education.

Stamp, P. (1989). *Technology, gender, and power in Africa.* Ottawa, ONT: IDRC.

Stamp, P. (1995). Mothers of invention: Women's agency in the Kenyan State. In L. Gardner (Ed.), *Provoking agents, gender and agency in theory and practice.* Chicago: University of Illinois Press.

The Women of the Veil (1992, July 11). *The Vancouver Sun,* pp. 1, 10.

WaThiong, N. (1984). *Decolonizing of the mind: The politics of language in African literature.* Nairobi: Heinemann.

Watt, S. and Cook, J. (1991). Racism: Whose liberation? Implications for women's studies. In J. Aaron and S. Walby (Eds.), *Out of the margins: Women's studies in the 90s* (pp. 130–142). London: Falmer Press.

Chapter 7

Lethal Labels:
Miseducative Discourse
about Educative Experiences[1]

_____

Sandra Monteath and Karyn Cooper

The Other Side of Labeling

_____

Linda Rossler

> When inquiry aims to know other people, categorization cannot substitute for understanding (Lorraine Code, 1991, p. 170).

Systemic educational violence wears many disguises. One of these is the identification and labeling of special needs students through "case histories" rather than "stories of experience." The widespread educational practice of identifying and labeling certain students as being at an educational disadvantage because of an accident of birth or development, or an unfortunate life situation is a means by which school authorities attempt to categorize students for ease of administration. Ostensibly, labels such as survivor of abuse, dyslexic, behavior disordered, or developmentally handicapped, help educators provide compensatory measures for learners in circumstances, or with conditions, that make acquiring a formal education problematic. However, instead of opening the door to a fuller experience of formal education, descriptive or diagnostic labels may close that door firmly.

111

The act of labeling, coupled with the experience of being labeled, sets an individual apart from the community of learners. Identifying a learner as someone with uncommon educational needs may open the way to special consideration or remediation, but it also makes her or him different from other learners: "abnormal." Educators tend to focus on the "abnormality," at the expense of the constellation of other qualities and abilities that make up the individual concerned. We see a "victim of sexual abuse" instead of an intelligent, articulate person; we see a "developmentally handicapped" child instead of a lively, loving little girl. When this happens, we reduce a learner "from a whole and usual person to a tainted, discounted one" (Goffman 1963, p. 3). The act of labeling, however well-intentioned, creates a stigma and any act of stigmatization is an act of violence. When a stigma keeps a learner from realizing her or his full educational potential, when it forces her or him into an educational dead end, it becomes an act of educational systemic violence.

Categories and labels are a technological response to the problem of human understanding. That educators rely so heavily on typologies and standardized measures to address and assess hindrances to educational achievement is consistent with our cultural presuppositions about the nature of knowledge and the qualities of authentic inquiry. Our society privileges scientific knowledge above other kinds, and its idea (and ideal) of inquiry is the notion of a detached observer discovering facts about an objective reality. Positivistic approaches expect human sciences—of which education is one—to mimic the exactness of what Edmund Husserl called the mathematical natural sciences (Husserl, 1970). We readily resort to classificatory investigations and reductionist analyses of experience. But what Husserl argued more than fifty years ago still holds today. He said that the methods of the mathematical natural sciences, of which classifying is one, and measurement another, are inappropriate for inquiring into and understanding human experience.

More recently, continental philosophers like Gadamer (1975), Anglo-American philosophers like Rorty (1991), and American educational researchers like Eisner (1991) have echoed Husserl's words. Feminist theorists like Code (1991), Oakley (1980), and Lather (1991) have added their voices to the chorus of critiques of positivist approaches to knowing ourselves and others. But our discipline has largely ignored the trenchant criticisms of natural science paradigms that have taken place in the last twenty or so years. We continue to employ those paradigms predominantly, not only in research, but in our pedagogy.

Learning the value of labels that identify and describe defects and deficits in a learner is part of our training; applying labels, often unreflectively, is part of our practice. For an instructor, the process of identifying, categorizing, and labeling brings a semblance of order to what would otherwise be an undifferentiated throng of students. Labeling is thus a practice of considerable convenience and utility.

As Rossler will argue in the second half of this chapter, as long as we remain mindful of what we are doing when we use labels, the practice of labeling is not necessarily harmful. However, difficulties arise when we confuse the act of differentiating one student from another by means of categories and labels with the acquisition of authentic knowledge and understanding about our students. At this point, because they delude us, labels do harm. But when labels blind us to "the suffering, afflicted, fighting, human subject" (Sacks 1987, viii), when they prevent us from recognizing the complexity of an individual's situation and the ingenuity and creativity with which she or he has responded to it and turn a living subject into an object of scrutiny, labels become instruments of educational systemic violence, and truly lethal.

Objectifying Experience

A quantitative measure for determining the degree of suffering that sexual abuse caused its victims was presented at a recent conference. Presumably, an educational psychologist using the measure would be able to take the case history of the client and compare the "facts" identified through history-taking and history-making on an itemized scale. It is quite likely that the items identified in the measure would influence the "facts" that the psychologist was finding. It is much less likely that the psychologist would recognize the way hidden biases—both those incorporated into the design of the measure, and her or his personal ones—would influence the findings. Not only are quantitative measures seen to be "objective" in themselves, but users have been trained to be "objective" and "detached." Observations are safely beyond the influence of either the texts the psychologist reads or the temperament she or he suppresses. Presumably, having constructed an "objective" case history based on equally "objective" measures, the psychologist would be able to make an "informed" choice as to treatment, and would be able also to predict its likely outcome.

This story of an educational psychologist attempting to use a quantitative measure for determining the degree of suffering that sexual abuse causes became our "toehold to inquiry" (Rorty, 1991). It pushed us to think about the widespread educational practice of categorizing and labeling students in ways that may make them prisoners of their pigeonholes, thus making public schooling a miseducative rather than an educative experience. Four related concerns came to mind:

1. The assumption that an affliction can be measured according to a quantitative scale. Neither hurt nor healing can be so measured. A quantitative measure gives us information; it does not give us insight.

2. The person devising the scale is a possessor of professional power (Code, 1991). Any evaluation of suffering that an educational psychologist would do would count as valid knowledge in a way that any interpretation by the actual sufferer would not. The evaluation of "disorders" and "disabilities" thought to affect academic performance denies the expertise of the person who is having the experience and who thus knows best its impact on her or his life.

3. A quantified evaluation wears a mask of neutrality (Code, 1991) that conceals its ineluctable subjective dimension. Although deeply rooted in the subjectivities of those who invent them and those who implement them, quantitative evaluative procedures enact institutionalized objectivism (Code, 1991) through procedural objectivity (Eisner, 1991). In a society that privileges objectivity, to appear to be objective is to have power.

4. The quantification of experience excludes more than it includes. As Dorothy Smith (1990) has pointed out, the case histories

constructed by a possessor of professional power are highly selec-
tive documents in which the professional assembles "facts" according to the rules and conventions of the profession:

> (Case histories) ignore the contexts in which events, actions, ut-
> terances occurred, and conceal the observational and other work
> of those reporting as components in the making of the report
> (Smith, 1990, p. 100).

Let us put these concerns into context through the story of a child
measured and found wanting by an educational psychologist.

Alana

Alana, a winsome little girl who brightens the lives of everyone she meets, is the five-year-old daughter of Lesley, a teacher.
Alana's label was "pervasive developmental delay." When school
authorities decided that Alana should undergo psychological assessment, Lesley believed that the educational psychologist had already predetermined that Alana was autistic. Thus, when the
psychologist met Alana, she interpreted Alana's behavior in a way
that confirmed her preliminary diagnosis. When Alana remembered the rules about going with strangers and showed anxiety
about leaving her mother, the psychologist described her as
"clingy." When Alana refused to do a puzzle of blocks, and instead
lined them up in a row, the psychologist described her as "unco-
operative." A different "possessor of professional power" might
have described her as creative. Lesley's child seemed to be an entirely different child from the child that the psychologist saw. For
example, Alana was in the habit of making her own breakfast. Lesley saw this as evidence of a desirable independence; the psychologist saw it as evidence of antisocial behavior.

A psychologist is in a position of privilege vis-à-vis the interpretation of a child's behaviour. How Lesley experienced Alana, and
how Alana saw herself, counted for nothing. Fortunately for Alana,
not all psychologists assess the same child in the same way. A second psychologist strongly disagreed with his colleague. He said that
the first report was inaccurate and unfair, and he talked with (not

at) Alana and her mother to help him understand how the world looked from Alana's point of view. His insight opened the way to a happy ending to Alana's story.

The systemic violence of this instance was allayed only because Lesley was a teacher. She was able to use the second psychological assessment to nullify the first, and to select a school with a good program for Alana. Had Leslie not been a teacher, and in that sense a possessor of professional power in her own right, the outcome of this story would have been different. Others do not have such an opportunity. The systemic aspect of the violation is more dangerous to members of society without access to professional power. For many children, the potential for a label to be lethal is doubled because parents, too, are labeled by circumstances of family (divorce, separation) or of economy (unemployed, working class, etc.).

Adults are sometimes able to overcome the effects of a label, but children are not so fortunate because they lack the necessary life experiences and political acumen. Their educational prospects may come to a violent end. Michael's story is a tragic case in point.

Michael

Michael developed epilepsy. In a few short months he passed from the world of "normal" human beings into the nether realm of the mentally handicapped. The final diagnosis, mental retardation, was like a death sentence—for him and his family. The label attached to him caused irreparable damage. He was excluded from his neighborhood public school and sent to a residential school where his "caregivers" abused him. He reacted with anger, but the resident psychologist described his anger as "inappropriate." As a result, another label was added: he was re-classified as "aggressive," drugged, and put in restraints. His cognitive abilities, at least those that were measurable, further declined.

Michael, like any human being, was a complex individual with many competencies. The label of "mentally handicapped with aggressive tendencies" precluded any understanding and appreciation of his complexity. Labels force people into pigeonholes, isolating them from others. In this way we deprive them of the interdependence and interconnection of the web of life. When we label we should consider that as we construct limiting images of others, so we construct ourselves as distorting and distorted mirrors of what we see (Caputo, 1987).

The stories of Michael and Alana illustrate the potential lethality of labels. It is our contention that the damage of being "different" would be minimized if those diagnosing the difference used "stories of experience" rather than traditional case studies.

Case Histories or Stories of Experience?

Neither a case history (clinical profile) nor a "story of experience" contains everything about an experience as lived. However, there are critical differences between case histories and stories of experience and these are relevant to our discussion of the lethal potential of labels.

Case histories are, by nature, oriented to disease, to deficit. They are products of the Hippocratic idea that "diseases have a course, from their first intimations to their climax or crisis, and thence to their happy or fatal resolution" (Sacks, 1987, p. vii). Psychologists do not usually take case histories of "healthy" or "normal" individuals. They take case histories of individuals who are in some way "un-healthy" or "ab-normal." The case history that a practitioner constructs presents details of a client's life thought to be relevant to the diagnosis. The disease or deficit determines what "facts" are included in the account, and what "facts" are omitted. Even the sequence in which the case history presents the "facts" functions as a set of instructions to the reader to understand the text in a certain way (Smith 1990). Smith describes case histories as ideological narratives.

Stories of experience, or what Smith calls primary narratives (1990), are told by, or on behalf of, the individual who underwent the experience being described. There is still a selection of "facts," for no narrative account can fully capture lived experience, but, it is the subject of, or participant in, the story and not a possessor of

professional power who makes the selection of "facts." The storyteller selects from a multiplicity of details·those that are appropriate to the theme.

The most crucial difference between case histories and stories
of experience is that the former are constructed to provide information about the ways in which an affliction has marked its sufferer, and the latter are constructed to give us insight into the
contextual experiences of another's life. Another important difference lies in the identity of the author. A case history is always written by someone other than the person who had the experience. A
story of experience is at least coauthored by the person who had the
experience. It is possible for a researcher or practitioner to negotiate the inferred meaning of an account of an experience with the
person who had the experience, and to arrive at an interpretation
that reflects and respects the perspectives of both (Oakley, 1980;
Lather, 1991). A case history is an ideological narrative that gets
much of its power from its assumed objectivity. A story of experience gets its power by admitting its subjectivity.

Conclusion

When we identify a child or adult learner as having special
needs, we should be careful that our identification does not turn
into stigmatization. To stigmatize is to aggravate an individual's
suffering and make her or his transcendence of it that much more
difficult. It is to engage in miseducative discourse about what could
be revisioned as an educative experience.

Labeling, which the practice of taking case histories supports,
reduces the complex web of an individual's life to a single, sullied
thread. Each time we use a label, each time we describe someone
as being damaged or deficient, each time we speak of some pathological condition as being the nature of a student, we must ask
what the label is preventing us from seeing. If a label is preventing
us from recognizing and respecting the mingled yarn of good and
ill that is any individual, then the label is harmful, and we need to
abandon it.

As an alternative or complement to evaluative procedures we suggest that part of our pedagogical practice should be to elicit stories of experience and listen to them. Through the power of stories, those whom we would otherwise reduce to objects for investigation and analysis reveal themselves as suffering, fighting human subjects worthy of our respect, consideration, and love.

If educators really want to understand the challenges that face learners in acquiring an education, and if we really want to help them become truly educated, at the very least we have to balance "scientific methods" with "narrative" approaches to understanding. Only by listening to the stories of experience can we hope to provide an education that helps fulfill individual needs and potential.

The Other Side
of Labeling

———

Linda Rossler

My daughter, Annette, was twelve years old when the bizarre behaviors became absolutely fearful. She ran away from home a number of times, hitchhiking to other provinces. She had attempted suicide more than once in a month. She lit candles and hid them in her closet. She stole entire boxes of cookies and other sweets from the cupboard, ate them in their entirety, and hid the empty containers under her bed. She started to write poems and stories that told of death and demonic happenings. She was hearing voices when no one was there. In addition, her principal was calling several times a month to tell me of another episode that Annette had initiated. I was very worried.

Annette had always been a good student. In grade three, standardized test scores indicated that she was three grade levels above her grade placement. Now she was failing miserably in several subjects. I had been to school to talk to her teachers about her behavior. The answers I received from the school included: she is looking for attention, joint custody is causing her insecurity, she is on a power trip, and she needs tough love. Her teacher indicated that, had Annette been up North on one of the reserves, her behavior would be considered quite "normal"—a reference to my daughter's adoption and Native heritage, which I found stereotypical and counterproductive.

I requested a psychological assessment be done through the school. The psychologist reported that Annette was of average intelligence. This did not explain the frightening behaviors, nor did it eliminate the pending danger. It did not even help to understand how better to deal with the change in my daughter.

Something was seriously wrong but no one else seemed to recognize the impending disaster. School officials attempted to provide intervention and follow-through, but their attempts at behavior modification and systematic monitoring were not enough. I was a special educator and a vice principal, so I was knowledgeable about the different routes for obtaining assistance. By the time I went for help from Child and Youth Services, the suicide attempts were up to five per month.

At Child and Youth Services, a psychiatrist found that Annette exhibited schizophrenic-like tendencies with psychosis. A biological trigger had been put into play by the hormone changes of puberty and the stress of family breakdown. These labels were familiar to me; finally, I understood where the bizarre behaviors were originating and knew there were interventions that could help.

Why Label?

The practice of labeling evolved from a psychomedical model which encompassed diagnosis, classification, and placement of students according to the unique and elusive characteristics that distinguish one group of individuals from another (Winzer, 1993). Research on its effects is discrepant and open to several interpretations. Though there may be some negative consequences associated with labeling, there are also reasons to continue the practice (Hallahan and Kauffman, 1989). Labeling

> permits us to identify children whose learning and behavioural characteristics cause them to require differentiated instruction. It is often a necessary administrative lever within the school system to obtain funding for special services. It can be helpful to parents, especially when a condition is initially diagnosed. For parents, the name of a handicap may seem to give them some control over it (Akerley, 1975, cited in Winzer, 1993).

Although many of the reasons for labeling are held in disdain by some, there are advantages that make them useful to parents, teachers and children: Classification can make the affliction more acceptable. Many parents, eager for a more euphemistic label for their children, adopt designations and classification that can result in increased visibility for groups of people with special needs. Classification can make others more tolerant of a disability. It may provide explanations for behavior or appearance for which people may otherwise be blamed or stigmatized (Feidler and Simpson, 1987). It can promote effective communication among agencies, services, and professionals that deal with individuals who are exceptional (Feidler and Simpson, 1987). Labels can help to alleviate peer stigmatization. Students with disabilities often experience isolation but this is often because of their behaviors not because of a label. Peers may find students "different" and shy away from them. The use of a label may provide an explanation which allows students to be more accepting. It also enables students to find others to associate with who are like them.

Some of the positive changes attributed to labeling occur on three levels. First, the labels provide a meaning or understanding of the true issue. Second, they eliminate feelings of inadequacy and guilt and replace them with positive feelings conducive to moving forward. Finally, they contribute directly to swift interventions and alternative procedures for helping the child.

Gerber (1991) found that there was a need for cognitive, affective and behavioral alignment in determining the most effective therapeutic approach for working with clients. When these three are aligned, children feel that they receive the help they need and can understand what is happening to them. Feelings about the problem can be moved from fear and isolation to encouragement, especially if children are involved in planning intervention and goal setting. When change occurs in meaning, feeling, and acting, the most productive interventions can be implemented. But individual consideration of need is fundamental to intervention.

The use of labels allows for input from experts in areas beyond the scope of the general educator. The more severe the need, the greater the necessity for alternate strategies of intervention. In severe cases, intervention may require intercessions outside of education. Schooling may in fact become secondary to emotional needs if the student is to be truly helped.

Labeling is about determining the exact needs of the student and making sure those specific needs are met within the most enabling environment. The child's behavior can then be viewed as a symptom of a more serious medical problem rather than as a willful misdemeanor. For example, once a student is identified as a person with a learning disability, teachers reconsider their previous assessment of the child as "lazy, poorly behaved and inattentive."

The labeling process is essential for the accurate assessment of need, which is crucial for proper intervention. Without it the educational system suffers from client perception of lack of effectiveness. The more serious the case, the greater the need for identification. Even though all students are alike in terms of their need for love, safety, and security, students with severely challenging conditions are more likely to be helped when the specific need is identified.

The use of a label can refocus students, educators, and parents. They are beneficial when they are used to address questions directly related to providing immediate assistance. When considering the use of labels, educators must consider these ethical questions:

1. Will labeling result in a better understanding of the nature of the challenging condition?

2. Will it facilitate the removal of debilitating feelings?

3. Will it speed up the intervention process?

4. Will additional resources be allocated as a result?

5. Will it allow professionals, parents and students to work better together?

I do not deny Monteath and Cooper's contention that the misuse of labels can be damaging. When they are used to objectify a person so that decision makers are detached from and disinterested in the person and they deal only with the actions without emotion and caring, then it is counterproductive. However, this objectification is the issue that needs to be addressed and not the use of labels itself.

In arguing for labeling, I find a similar frustration to the one Monteath and Cooper used in arguing against it. Many parents walk away from the education system with an empty feeling and a sense of hopelessness—whether their child with difficulties has been labeled or not. Some are fortunate enough to know where there are other doors to knock on, but many parents do not have access to these resources.

Teachers and administrators attempt to make the school environment the best possible for all students, but there are still children whose needs are not being met. Educators need quality information upon which to make good decisions. For student needs to be accurately addressed, some form of identification is necessary.

Labels as Systemic Violence

If institutionalized practices and procedures that adversely impact upon disadvantaged individuals constitute systemic violence, labels have the potential to be systemically violent. The direct impact of systemic violence results in frustration and powerlessness. These feelings are experienced by students, parents, teachers, and school administrators. People involved with special students do not always recognize the issues associated with systemic violence. It is only on reflection that these practices will become visible as impacting negatively on an individual with severe needs and those associated with them. Labels are systemically violent if they lack the following:

1. Attention to individual needs. Students with special needs must always be treated as individuals in spite of any labels which might be used to aid in diagnosis and intervention.

2. Attention to voice. Students and parents must be involved throughout the labeling process. The hierarchy of "credible voices" has to be eliminated.

3. Recognition that "acceptable and appropriate practices" do not always address the real issue. Educators must be alert to new practices and innovative solutions.

4. Consistency in meeting needs not in meeting protocol. The protocol of "diagnosis" is not as important as addressing the needs of the student within the context of her/his life experiences.

Note

1. An earlier version of this chapter was presented to the Canadian Association for the Study of Women and Education as part of the Canadian Society for the Study of Education Conference in Calgary, Alberta, Canada, June 1994.

References

Caputo, J. (1987). *Radical hermeneutics: Repetition, deconstruction, and the hermeneutic project*. Bloomington: Indiana University Press.

Code, L. (1991). *What can she know? Feminist theory and the construction of knowledge*. Ithaca: Cornell University Press.

Eisner, E. (1991). *The enlightened eye: Qualitative inquiry and the enhancement of educational practice*. New York: Macmillan Publishing Co.

Feidler, C. R. and Simpson, R. I. (1987). Modifying the attitudes of nonhandicapped high school students toward handicapped peers. *Exceptional Children, 53*, 342–349.

Gadamer, H. (1975). *Truth and method*. Translated by C. Barden and J. Cumming. New York: The Seabury Press.

Gerber, S. (1991). *Responsive therapy and personal commitment: Integrative models*. Paper presented at the Annual Conference of the Western Association for Counselor Education and Supervision, San Diego, CA.

Goffman, E. (1963). *Stigma: Notes on the management of spoiled identity*. Englewood Cliffs: Prentice Hall.

Hallahan, D. and Kauffman, J. (1986). *Exceptional children*. Toronto: Prentice Hall.

Husserl, E. (1970). *The crisis of European sciences and transcendental phenomenology*. Translated by David Carr. Evanston, ILL: Northwestern University Press.

Lather, P. (1991). *Getting smart: Feminist research and pedagogy with/in the postmodern*. New York: Routledge.

Milich, R. et al. (1992). Effects of stigmatizing information on children's peer relations. *School Psychology Review*, *21* (3), 400–409.

Ministry of Supply and Services, Ottawa. (1993). *Final report of the Canadian panel on violence against women*. Ottawa: Government of Canada.

Oakley, A. (1980) Interviewing women. In Helen Robers (Ed.), *Doing feminist research*. London: Routledge & Kegan Paul.

Rorty, R. (1991). *Objectivism, relativism, and truth. Philosophical Papers, Volume 1*. Cambridge: Cambridge University Press.

Sacks, O. (1987). *The man who mistook his wife for a hat*. New York: Harper & Row.

Smith, D. (1990). *The conceptual practices of power: A feminist sociology of knowledge*. Toronto: University of Toronto Press.

Walker, L. (1979). *The battered woman*. New York: Harper & Row.

Winzer, M. (1993). *Children with exceptionalities*. Scarborough, ON: Prentice Hall.

Part III

Systemic Violence,
Women, and Teachers

Chapter 8

The Family Romance
and the
Student-Centered Classroom[1]

Lisa Jadwin

Buried in the 1994 *Chronicle of Higher Education Almanac* is an essential piece of information: fully 30.2 percent of male and 24.2 percent of female first-year students "agree strongly or somewhat" that "married women's activities are best confined to home and family" (Attitudes and characteristics of freshmen, 1993, p. 17). How do such attitudes affect the authority of female professors who share the age group or status of "married women"? To students, the "woman/scholar" occupies the body, age group, and status of a "mother," but operates in the public sphere of a college or university—traditionally the territory of the metaphorical father, the intellectual mentor who prepares his youthful charges for adult participation in the public sphere. This bizarre hybrid resembles neither the nurturing Mother of students' primary and secondary school experience nor the demanding and learned Father whom they expect to encounter behind the lectern. Consequently, students taught to believe that women belong in the private sphere are confused: How should they respond to a female professor? Should she be respected and obeyed as an authority—that is, an educated, articulate professional? Or is it all right to despise and even undermine her as an impostor?

Students' confusion about the authority status of female professors stems from a variety of factors related to basic gender stereotyping. Here, however, I would like to focus on how the implementation of a "student-centered" pedagogy further undermines a female professor's classroom authority. Many female professors, especially those who identify themselves as feminists, practice student-centered pedagogy because it is fundamentally democratic, designed to empower rather than to indoctrinate students. Students, however, are likely to perceive decentered authority models as "no authority at all," a deviation from the lecturing norm and possibly evidence of the professor's incompetence. Consequently, the female professor who opts to use student-centered pedagogy further compromises an authority that many of her students already view as shaky.

Student-Centered Pedagogy

The female professor who practices student-centered pedagogy faces a double bind: her refusal to assume absolute authority over her students threatens to undermine what little authority she already possesses. If she opts to buttress her shaky authority by adopting authoritarian pedagogical models, she faces another double bind. By indoctrinating students rather than involving them actively in the creation of meaning, the female professor threatens to recapitulate the dichotomous authority structures that have been used to exclude women like herself from the academy. So what should the female professor do? Theoretically, she should be able to subvert the double binds by striking a balance between the stereotypic pedagogical extremes of permissiveness and tyranny, borrowing freely from both traditions while leaning heavily on neither. In my experience, however, merging the two pedagogical styles (for example, by combining lecturing and collaborative learning) has succeeded only in upper-division courses, where students tend to bring more maturity, motivation, and expertise to the table.

In lower-level courses—particularly introductory writing courses—my attempts to balance or combine pedagogies have been less successful. They generally meet with continued inappropriate challenges to my authority as well as unusual levels of resistance to the goals and process of the class. Though frustrating to teach, these courses have taught me that students' resistance to female authority and student-centered teaching may have as much to do with psychological family dynamics as with broader patterns of gender stereotyping. The dynamics of my students' resistance to my authority and pedagogical style strongly resemble the psychological dynamics of the Freudian/Lacanian "family romance," (Lacan, 1977) a phenomenon that links children's successful transition into adulthood—a realm of abstract symbolic discourses— with their ability to reject or repress an archetypal mother who represents prelinguistic consciousness. This chapter explores this dynamic, first by outlining the gendered implications of student-centered teaching and the family romance itself, then by relating my students' behavior and comments to these two paradigms.

My students are deeply habituated to what Paulo Freire has called the "banking" epistemology of education, the model that dominates American higher education from the SAT to the GRE. Freire (1970) significantly uses a sexual metaphor to describe his "banking" paradigm: knowledge is an object possessed by a male teacher who impresses it on students who must simply sit there and "take it" (pp. 67–68). Ideologically the process models indoctrination if not intellectual rape, and is an apt paradigm for the way one group of people learns to dominate another. Certainly it is both hierarchical and patriarchal.

Student-centered pedagogy, in contrast, is intrinsically anti-hierarchical, an openly politicized strategy for empowering the least vocal members of a group. As Frances Maher (1985) points out, student-centered pedagogy is designed to involve

> students in constructing and evaluating their own education. It assumes that each student has legitimate rights and potential contributions to the subject-matter. Its goal is to enable students to draw on their personal and intellectual experiences to build a satisfying version of the subject, one that they can use productively in their own lives. Its techniques involve students in the assessment and production, as well as the absorption, of the material. The teacher is a major contributor, a creator of structure and a delineator of issues, but not the sole authority (p. 30).

Ideally student-centered pedagogy encourages students to help create meaning in the classroom. This goal, however, often seems counterintuitive to students habituated to the banking paradigm. In student-centered classrooms, where authority becomes fluid, both teaching and learning become improvisatory and contingent. Questions about evaluation arise on both sides: How, for example, should professors measure students' progress, and how should students fill out computerized teaching evaluations that ask them to rate the professor's "lectures"? What information or skills are important, and how will students be tested on them? How will expertise be recognized in the classroom? How will students learn to judge the good or true from the bad or false? At what point, if ever, will the professor—that "creator of structure and delineator of issues"—take charge and "cover" material monologically?

These questions should and can be negotiated between teacher and students as a matter of course. In practice, however, they require a constant rethinking of banking-paradigm pedagogy, including issues of power and authority. Though I would like to believe that students want to be stimulated and transformed by student-centered teaching, my students are ambivalent about liberationist pedagogy. Many prefer the banking system, which is predictable and allows them to remain intellectually passive and emotionally detached from learning. Many resent the level of responsibility and involvement student-centered teaching requires of them. Consequently, student-centered classrooms, particularly writing classrooms, are hardly utopian, but fraught with resistance and rebellion. Students quickly discover that they can alter the progress of a student-centered class by withholding participation, refusing to work, or insulting the professor. Furthermore, resistance and rebellion are difficult for the teacher to handle because of the putatively cooperative nature of the enterprise. In the "banking" classroom the professor is armed with The Grade, which can be wielded as a weapon against reluctant, lazy, or insubordinate students. But since student-centered teaching offers students options instead of absolutes, they know that their response—no matter what it may be—must be honored.

My students respond to the decentering of authority in the student-centered classroom in three primary ways. Some accept it initially in good faith, agreeing to participate and to concentrate on acquiring skills rather than information. Others tune out, participating as marginally as possible. Still others rebel, attempting to restore the familiar "banking" paradigm they prefer. Most proceed through these positions in stages as the semester proceeds. But most of my students, though initially attracted by the course design, ultimately reject the methodology ostensibly designed to "liberate" them. This rejection stems from their epistemological assumptions about both education and gender. Because they define authority as absolute, oppressive, and masculine, a woman assuming a position of power must be masquerading at best, unnatural at worst. Student-centered pedagogy ironically throws this into relief. Not only does a woman lack any real authority to begin with, but by running a student-centered classroom she tries to give away her "lack" to the students. To them this looks like a disease disguised as a gift. Neither a female professor nor other students, according to their paradigm, has access to the symbolic order they equate with formal education. Consequently, what could possibly go on in a student-centered class that could be of use to them now or after they graduate? Why should they listen to me or to each other?

Family Romance

My students' epistemological prejudices are exacerbated by their collective psychological moment: I have not used the word "familiar" naively to describe their unquestioned acceptance of the primacy of "banking" pedagogy. Most of my eighteen to twenty-two-year-old students are literally in the process of attempting to separate from their primary caregiver mothers. Their mothers, along with surrogates like nuns and elementary school teachers, are the only female authorities my students have ever known. The other women they "respect"—actresses and models—are conveniently mute and thus possess only a specularized kind of sexual power. Products of a culture that refuses even to call child rearing "work," few are prepared to accord authority to women who nurture and instruct children, and they are ready to enact their resentment towards and fear of such women onto their female professors in the form of transference.

These students are attending college in pursuit of entry into a formal manifestation of the symbolic order—the academy—a realm of specifically patriarchal power grounded in language. Significantly, the Oedipal drama (Freud, 1953) plays out most dramatically in my writing courses among students whose writing skills are painfully underdeveloped. Traditional-aged students manage their transitions from a nearly prelinguistic reliance on their mothers to entry into the powerful, word-wielding (that is, word-writing) world of their fathers, by forcing me to enact both corners of the triangle. This identity-transformation—a transformation uniquely facilitated by my ambiguous status as woman/expert—allows students to play out their Oedipal conflicts and to enforce their and my entry into the phallogocentric symbolic order with a vengeance.

The drama that is played out in my student-centered classrooms closely echoes the family romance. A sketch or outline of the process looks like this: Early in the term, I am their all-loving, accepting mother who is interested in what they have to say and does not enforce knowledge autocratically upon them. Then, once the first grades or conflicts arise in the class, they begin to resent this motherly stance, acting out in ways that beg punitive responses—refusing to participate and complete assignments, for example—actions that force me to enact the part of the phallic mother, the punitive half-possessor of the phallus. Then, often through outright acts of insubordination, they force me to enjoin rules of the banking paradigm, transforming me into an imitation father who withholds, punishes, demands, is "objective" and objectifying. Certainly the logic of the American college classroom enables this; the law of the father is embodied in that most potent of classroom signs, the grade—the symbol of phallogocentric mastery.

Most of my students initially embrace the maternalistic aspect of the class's subjectivist epistemology. Consciously or unconsciously they recognize that an inclusive pedagogy reflects a feminine or feminist epistemology, the nurturant ethic Sara Ruddick (1980) has called "maternal thinking." Initially, many are attracted to this apparent anti-structure, relieved to escape the "banking" paradigm and ready to return to a childlike state of unselfconscious exploration. They report: "This is the only really fun class I have," "I never know what's going to happen in here, so I don't get bored," "My ideas are valued here." Some say they feel newly free to speak and write. Many, however, remain silent, watchful: unsure of my expectations and accustomed to betrayal by authorities, they fear everything might vanish instantly; they refuse to become subjects in some eccentric pedagogical experiment. At this early point in the term, the female professor is still "mother," the other-directed, nonverbal (silent, speech-honoring) parent who affirms feelings and intuitions. My students enjoin me to nurture their sometimes regressively narcissistic subjectivity (which arises as endless pointless whining about and refusing to read challenging texts, repeated requests to sleep and eat disruptively in class, obsessive preoccupation with personal problems, inability or refusal to focus on a text or issue). Since language exists in this "stage" of the student-centered classroom, I hesitate to identify it with Lacan's (1977) imaginary, but my students' emphasis on "feelings" rather than "thought" when they talk about the class is surely significant. So is the student-centered class's emphasis on collaboration, which partly effaces or engulfs students' emotional and intellectual boundaries. To my students, the "learning" produced at this stage has little clear ownership or definable form—as one student put it, "not things you take notes on."

The moment at which learning becomes attributed, owned, marked (specifically with students' names and grades) inaugurates an irrevocable change in the student-centered class. In the act of handing back grades or evaluations, the female professor exposes herself as an impostor, a phallic mother who pretends to offer the almost prelinguistic acceptance of the imaginary, but invokes the symbolic order to measure student "progress." Students' uncomplicated identification with the maternal has been destroyed; the female professor has substituted symbolic judgment for the visual, discursive affirmation (even mirroring) typical of classroom interactions, and the signifiers she has chosen usually inscribe "lack." To students, this is a simple betrayal: since they view "mothers" by definition as nonjudgmental—fathers "discipline" errant children in their families—a woman who imposes discipline has betrayed her role. A mother would never be so stern, so "demanding and judgmental," as one student told me, continuing: "You could learn a few things from my mother about how to act."

My students, having in the past been punished for challenging authority directly, typically express their rage at this betrayal passive-aggressively. The chaos that infiltrates the classroom in the following weeks takes a variety of forms and depends on individual personalities and group dynamics, which of course vary from class to class. But the rebellion always takes the following forms. Some students refuse to complete writing assignments; on many days, a majority of class members have not completed the readings; still others, often the majority of the class, refuse altogether to participate in class discussion and sit silently with expressions of resentment, watching the clock. A few students interrupt me, talk while I am talking, and/or attack my decisions and opinions with ridicule or open hostility. Significantly, their characteristic attempts to block the progress of the class are linguistic; all involve producing inappropriate or disruptive words or refusing to provide words at all. (As a metaphorical echo of toilet training, the situation is almost laughable.)

The loss of the maternal imaginary is reflected in these little enactments of separation—students' ways of asserting their autonomy and repressing and reconstructing their pain into indirect and typically linguistic forms. Of course this facilitates their transition into the symbolic order. Rejecting the fluidity of their former identities, they work to establish themselves as "tough," "hard," "mean," and often aggressive. They sabotage both large and small-group discussions, which they now freely disparage as "a waste of time" or "stupid," simply by refusing to speak. (It is interesting that my female students display little differentiation from male students in their actualization of the Lacanian paradigm. Ironically, the brightest of them typically embrace the phallogocentric model of academic achievement unquestioningly, and are often eager to dissociate themselves from what Belenky et al. (1986) have called "women's ways of knowing," which these female students regard as "wimpy" and inferior.)

These actions and nonactions have a disruptive effect on the classroom; all of them bring student participation to a grinding halt. My attempts to call attention to and analyze the difficulties only serve to clarify the aporia that has become the unspeakable subject of the course. Since in every course I am ostensibly teaching an academic subject like writing or postmodern exile narratives or Victorian poetry, at this juncture I usually face two options. The first is to preserve the student-centered structure of the course and proceed in spite of the students' refusal to participate. Sometimes I ask students to write; sometimes I come in and simply sit down at a desk in the back of the room and ask a student to take over; sometimes I ask opening questions, sit waiting for responses, and after a couple of minutes get out a book and read until someone decides to speak. Students' responses eventually become so attenuated that the class becomes, in the words of one colleague, like "mental dental work." I begin to dread showing up for class; I find myself watching the clock; I find it difficult to remain patient with the students and to respect them, since their passive-aggressive resistance, even when pointed out to them, persists until it is nearly tangible. On such days, I think of giving up teaching altogether.

But that's the point, isn't it? It is also, usually the turning point. Exhausted and frustrated, I give up trying to pull things out of them, and start talking more. The rationalizations one can make for this are endless, but they begin with "I want to make it easier on myself and give them what they want," and usually end with "I have to cover a certain amount of material," all of which are, in practice, antithetical to the aims of the student-centered classroom. Talking devolves into lectures; with relief on their faces they get out their notebooks and start taking notes. The students start doing the reading; participation picks up though they still refuse to work together effectively in small groups. I swoop down on the ones who continue to behave disruptively, taking them aside and dressing them down, ordering them to behave more respectfully of me and others in the classroom, reading them the proverbial riot act. Instead of resenting this and making further challenges, to my eternal surprise, they seem to enjoy it, expect it. And why not? They have effected the desired metamorphosis; the phallic mother has publicly demonstrated her desire for the phallus by taking on the role of father—enforcer of rules, setter of standards, upholder of "rigor," with all the phallic mastery that favorite academic adjective implies. The efficacy of the familiar banking paradigm—and, more important, of the symbolic order the banking paradigm manifests—has been reaffirmed because it has been restored. The students have repressed what they call the "touchy-feely"—the maternal. Their conviction that women lack authority has been confirmed, along with their confidence in their ability to control female behavior.

The personal cost of this classroom "drama" is substantial. My colleagues and I spend hours outside of class thinking about how to "make it work," blaming ourselves for the failure of our pedagogical strategies and trying to think up solutions to what we now simply call "the authority problem." We recognize that we are facilitating a psychological transformation that may have nothing to do with our courses' putative subjects; we know that students often learn much from interactions that seem horrendous at the time they happen.

We recognize that we are caught up in a transitional cultural period in which these problems with authority and transference affect all women in authority to some degree. We know that these dramas are particularly virulent at our college because of the institutional environment, our students' psychosocial backgrounds, and our own relative lack of status as faculty members (we are all assistants or associates). Surely, we also contribute to the drama by supplying countertransference. I have expressed my own rage at my feminine position of exclusion by browbeating the most insolently patriarchal of my pupils. The "father" stage of the triangulation provides a certain relief for exhausted faculty members as well as for students.

Though these factors mitigate the apparent futility of the situation, none helps us solve the problem of how to run student-centered classrooms. How, as women and scholars, can we avoid the process of "denying, absorbing, and being absorbed" by an epistemological system that we know to be subtly cooptative and ultimately oppressive—for ourselves and for our students?

Note

1. A previous version of this paper was included in the proceedings of the Conference of the American Association of University Women, Orlando, Florida, June 1995.

References

Aisenberg, N. and Harrington, M. (1988). *Women of academe: Outsider in the sacred grove*. Amherst, MA: University of Massachusetts.

Attitudes and Characteristics of Freshmen. (1993, August 25). *Chronicle of Higher Education Almanac*, p. 15.

Belenky, M., Clinchy, B., Goldberger, N. and Tarule, J. (1986). *Women's ways of knowing: The development of self, voice and mind*. New York: Basic Books.

Culley, M. and Portuges, C. (Eds.) (1985). *Gendered subjects: The dynamics of feminist teaching.* New York: Routledge.

Freire, P. (1970). *Pedagogy of the oppressed.* Translated by M. B. Ramos. New York: Seabury .

Freud, Sigmund (1953). *The Interpretation of Dreams.* Ed. James Strachey; trans. James Strachey et al. Vols. III, IV, and V of *The Standard Edition of the Complete Psychological Works of Sigmund Freud (24 vols.)* London: Hogarth.

Friedman, S. S. (1985). Authority in the feminist classroom—a contradiction in terms? In M. Culley and C. Portuges (Eds.), *Gendered subjects: The dynamics of feminist teaching* (pp. 203–8). New York: Routledge.

Kanter, E. M. (1977). *Men and women of the corporation.* New York: Basic Books.

Lacan, Jacques (1977). *Ecrits: A Selection.* Trans. Alan Sheridan. New York: W. W. Norton.

Lakoff, R. (1975). *Language and woman's place.* New York: Harper & Row.

Maher, F. (1985). Classroom pedagogy and the new scholarship on women. In M. Culley and C. Portuges (Eds.), *Gendered subjects: The dynamics of feminist teaching* (pp. 29–48). New York: Routledge.

Maher, F. (1985). Classroom pedagogy and the new scholarship on women. In M. Culley & C. Portuges (Eds.), *Gendered subjects: The dynamics of feminist teaching* (pp. 29–48). New York: Routledge.

Ruddick, Sara (1980). Maternal thinking. *Feminist Studies* 6, 70–96.

Sandler, B. R. (1986). *The campus climate revisited: Chilly for women faculty, administrators, and graduate students.* Washington, DC: Project on the Status and Education of Women, Association of American Colleges.

Simeone, A. (1987). *Academic women: Working towards equality.* South Hadley, MA: Bergin & Garvey.

Spender, D. (1980). *Man made language.* London: Routledge & Kegan Paul.

Weis, L. (1990). *Working class without work: High school students in a de-industrializing economy.* New York: Routledge.

Chapter 9

Disrupting the Code of Silence:
Investigating Elementary Students
Sexually Harassing Their Teachers[1]

Elisabeth Richards

I couldn't believe it. When I was on lunch supervision today, some grade 5 kid ran up behind me and gave me a wedgie—the little bastard grabbed my ass. So I went down and told the principal about it and do you know what he said? He told me that if I had better control of my classes this behavior never would have happened (A Teacher).

I too had experienced personal incidents of sexual harassment (e.g., a male student drew a picture of me naked with a penis in my mouth) and had received similar bouts of verbal reprimands from my colleagues when I expressed concern. When I heard this story, I wondered if this was a systemic problem rather than some freakish, anomalous experience. It was only when the principal refused to acknowledge that this supposedly gender-neutral behavior was actually one of patriarchal assault, that I saw the once hidden contradictions—the mostly male principals who say they are there to help but will not; the female elementary teachers who know they must "keep their class under control" but do not have the means to do so; and the children who "naturally" want to learn yet react to teachers in violent ways.

As a researcher concerned with educational systemic violence, I am troubled that we may at times forget how the teacher is involved in complicated dynamics which may disempower her. The above incident shows how certain teachers may be caught between the actions of their students and their principals. In order to further our understanding of educational systemic violence we must include the possibility that not all the violence occurring is directed towards the student. A modification of the definition of "educational systemic violence" to include this complication would read as follows: Practices and procedures that prevent students from learning [and teachers from teaching], thus harming them. The principal's interpretation of the boy's assault, namely, that it was a result of the teacher's incompetence, made it possible for this student to believe that he could get away with this behavior, thus harming the teacher's legitimacy and therefore her ability to teach.

Rather than beginning our analysis by examining her classroom management skills, as this administrator would do, let us examine the current discursive forces that (1) led this teacher to conflate the discourse of childhood prank with one of sexual impropriety; (2) enabled this principal to read the child's action as resulting solely from a "management problem"; and (3) position subjects in ways that privilege certain readings while precluding others.

By probing how sexual harassment/assault against female teachers is informed by "common sense" assumptions about the nature of harassment, childhood, and "teaching-as-mothering," I hope to contribute to a better understanding of how the combination of these various discourses works to mask certain social actions and prevents people from recognizing this form of sexual abuse when it occurs in the school system.

Not all female elementary teachers have these experiences, but there are enough such experiences, especially among those who teach a marginalized subject (such as Core French), to merit a certain level of generalization. Other factors, such as class status, ethnic subjectivity, and sexual orientation, also complicate matters as they place many teachers in a compounded oppressive situation. Due to the limits of both space and my "lived experience," this will be a partial account of a larger and more complicated problem, the beginnings of a much needed critique of sexual harassment in the elementary school system.

Sexual harassment, as a discursive act, has been inscribed in many social discourses throughout our society. This analysis is concerned with how power is exercised through the institutionalized effects of particular discourses that work to displace certain experiences of female teachers in the schools, so it is necessary to examine those discursive fields which are specific to that context. It will be argued that the amalgamation of liberal-humanist legal discourse, pedagogic discourse, and the teacher-as-mother discourse, puts the teacher in a less than adequate position to deal with sexual harassment from elementary students. These discourses will be situated in their historical context in order to deconstruct some of the taken-for-granted assumptions that currently inform the experiences of female teachers in school.

Sexual Harassment Legally Defined

The term "sexual harassment" is a rather recent invention, informed by a second wave of feminism that was, in turn, primarily inscribed in the enlightenment discourse of individual rights (Weed, 1989, pp. ix–xxi). As women's consciousness-raising groups in the 1970s began to identify similarities in their experiences of rape and rape prevention, they named those parallel experiences as "sexual harassment" (Linn, 1992, pp. 106–123). These terms were then codified and inscribed in legislation:

> Every person who is an employee has a right to freedom from harassment in the workplace because of sex by his or her employer or agent of the employer or by another employee (Ontario Human Rights Code, R.S.O. 1990, Section 7 (2)).

Once legislation at the provincial level had officially deemed sexual harassment as illegal, school boards began to adopt this discourse via board policies in the early 1980s (Toronto Board of Education, 1992). Sexual harassment discourse is currently in circulation via school policies, so the question is: Why did neither the teacher, nor her principal, take up this discourse?

To answer this question, we need to know how sexual harassment policies are constituted and read in the context of the schools. There are two kinds of sexual harassment identified in school board policies: quid pro quo and poisoned environment (Nemni, 1992).

Quid pro quo, the type of harassment "that occurs most often," refers to a relationship involving people in positions of unequal status whereby one person has control over another's employment (Nemni, 1992). This is usually the boss who is in a position to "confer, grant, or deny a benefit" (Ontario Human Rights Code, 1990).

The second type of harassment, known as the poisoned environment, is sexual harassment between coworkers and nonemployees which "poisons" the work environment (Nemni, 1992). The standard used to classify the perpetrator's conduct as harassment is, in both instances, based on the "reasonable person" standard (Riger, 1991). That is to say, the potential offender's culpability depends on whether or not a "reasonable" person would view the conduct as unwelcome. Hence, only when a sexual advance which "is known, or ought reasonably to have been known, by the person making the advance, to be unwanted by the recipient, can the charge of harassment be laid" (Nemni, 1992). [A discussion of the "reasonable woman" standard is found in Watkinson, chapter 1].

Liberal discourse, in its insistence on "individual rights," obscures the fact that "real harassment" only occurs when the victim "makes it known" to the perpetrator that the behavior is unwelcome. This deflects attention away from the damaging material effects of the act, and displaces it onto the victim's attempts to prevent it (Mani, 1992). With so much emphasis on the harassee's attempt to dissuade the harasser, and so little on the cruelty of the act itself, one may indeed ask whose rights are actually being protected? When statistics tell us that 88 percent of the people who are sexually violated are women, and that 25 percent of nearly all sex offenders are under the age of eighteen, it would seem that females in general, and female teachers in particular, are not the ones who benefit from such protection (Holden, cited in Briskin, 1990). By keeping the same epistemic structures of liberal humanism intact, whereby denying systemic differentials in power, male privilege is reconsolidated under the rubric of "minority rights" (Luke, 1992). In a discourse which implicitly frames male interests at the center, it is little wonder that the principal blamed the male student's action of harassment on the teacher's inability to keep "class control."

Even when the harassee makes it known to the harasser that his actions are "unwelcome," it does not guarantee that the law will interpret this behavior as sexual harassment. When Nemni (1992) outlines all the rights and freedoms that everyone should enjoy in the workplace, she stipulates, paradoxically, that not everyone can be accommodated by such definitions. The standard is not flexible enough to consider what the complainant feels. Some people are more sensitive than the norm. This extra sensitivity does not mean a sexual harassment complaint will have a greater chance of being supported. The measure is the norm, the "average" person (Nemni, 1992).

From a poststructural viewpoint, oversensitivity becomes a sign placed in binary opposition to lesser sensitivity, where its presence can be read as a lack of, rather than evidence of, harassment (Walkerdine, 1990). When the legal discourse offered in school policies constructs the "normal" person as less sensitive, that is, as more willing to see a student's sexual assault as a childish prank and thus as harmless rather than as a violation of self, the complaints of "overly sensitive" individuals can be seen as illegitimate. Hence, the binary of oversensitivity embedded in the legal construction of harassment can be used to undermine a teacher's plea for protection or retribution.

Viewing this problem from any one single discourse grossly oversimplifies its complexity. The problem as situated in a nexus of discourses that define real victims as actively trying to prevent the harassers' behavior while, simultaneously, not displaying the pathological behaviour of oversensitivity. If her allegations are read as being "oversensitive," she risks being positioned outside the harassment script (Marcus, 1992). She could be invalidated through discursive practices which construct her as an irrational female and, therefore, not capable of discerning between violent and nonviolent acts. Or she can be accused of being a perpetrator of another type of violence: making false accusations about innocent males—an alternative, yet equally undermining, discursive practice. Both form a classic Catch 22 situation. The teacher is caught in the web of silencing ideologies imbricated within various administrative and patriarchal discourses. The paralyzing effects of these proscriptive, regulatory labels leave little room for teacher resistance, since her account of the action will not be accepted.

Sexual harassment is primarily a repressive exercise of power from above (Walkerdine, 1990). The "normal" harasser is likely to hold more institutional power than the harassee. Such monolithic definitions of power ignore the unstable subjectivity which renders female teachers "at one moment powerful and at another power-less" (Walkerdine, 1990, p. 3). While the positioning of harassees in the legal discourse gives female teachers a certain degree of power to claim their victimized institutional status as employee, it simul-taneously renders them ineligible to claim their victimized status in the teacher-pupil discourse, where they are positioned as power-ful. The female teacher's own experience, which deviates from the standard form of harassment by one who has power, might be in-terpreted by others as an indication of her pathology (that is, an "incompetent teacher") rather than as an effect of social relations which have helped produce and define "normal" harassment (Walk-erdine, 1990). Perhaps this explains why the principal was able to read the teacher's situation as a defect in her abilities which he la-beled as "insufficient control over the class."

The "Child" in Pedagogic Discourse

Legal conceptions of "harassers" pose limitations on a teacher's reading of her own harassment. Teachers and principals are also subject to the discourse of the classroom which produces additional terms and categories in which they understand them-selves as teachers and the children as learners. Given the current production of "the child" in the pedagogic discourse, teachers come to read the sexual acts of children as childhood pranks rather than as acts of assault or violation (Walkerdine, 1990).

"The child" can be read differently depending on the context in which the term is inserted. The authoritarian teaching practices at the beginning of this century have gradually been replaced in favor of "progressive education" (Walkerdine, 1990). Overregimentation in both child rearing and current educational practices was said to be partly responsible for the rise of totalitarianism so education needed to develop a pedagogy which controlled citizens but did not regiment them (Walkerdine, 1990).

By the beginning of the century, there had been several chal-lenges to the overt authority of pedagogy in schools (Walkerdine, 1990). Froebel, Owen and Pestalozzi had touted the benefits of an "education according to nature" (Walkerdine, 1990). The influence of Darwin's scientific method shifted attitudes from a belief in an education according to nature to one infused with new scientific meanings (Weber, 1984). Using scientific techniques and principles, the needs of pupils could be revealed through direct study of children in naturalistic settings where they could develop at their own pace. Rather than being coerced into doing things they did not want to do, students would be allowed to choose. The pedagogy of choice was further influenced by the ideals of Piaget and Freud. Piaget believed that the goal of pedagogy was to create rational individuals who could govern themselves. He felt that "the love of beautiful bodies was to be left behind in childhood" (Piaget, 1977; cited by Walkerdine, 1990, p. 72). Since Freudian psychoanalysis viewed repression of childhood sexuality (based on a male standard) as unhealthy, the new pedagogy sought its expression. In this way, (male) children could pursue their quest toward the rational ideal, unimpeded by emotion and sexuality (Walkerdine, 1990).

Ironically, the discourse which was aimed to set (male) children free from the overregulation of the authoritarian classroom, helped to restrict (female) teachers' abilities to read sexually aggressive behaviour as anything other than a harmless expression of natural childhood sexuality. If all their actions were natural expressions of something, if sexuality was "just one of those things" to be worked out to allow the rational mind to take over, then the student's action was normal. It could not be read through the feminist critiques of patriarchal objectification and commodification of women. If one can expose the damaging aspects of "naturally expressive" child behavior, one can argue that the child should be seen as the agent of a violating act rather than as an innocent child passing through a phase of youthful overzealousness.

This is not to suggest that the discourse of the child-centered pedagogy explicitly described the child as sexually active. While children are allowed to express themselves through actions partly spawned from irrational sexual urges, expressions of sexuality which occur on school grounds are not discussed. Sex education courses focus on issues of disease prevention and pregnancy. Conversations encouraging the use of condoms "when the time comes" do not exactly deal with the issues of sexual harassment. In fact, a considerable amount of energy in schools is expended on desexualizing the child through texts that are hygienic and devoid of sexuality (Rose, cited in Walkerdine, 1990). So while "imagination" and "discovery" are given access in the discursive space constituted for the "child," "sexuality" must be kept safely contained. For example, sex education classes are taught by female teachers whose passions have been safely transformed into the asexual quality of maternal love. They are kept to the margins of school discourses, lest it interfere with the (male) child's quest toward rational adulthood.

The positioning of the teacher as the nurturing asexual Madonna figure protected by social taboos of incest, further reduces her ability to effectively deal with children's acts of sexual innuendo, harassment, or assault. Playing the mother figure adds to this thickening soup of paralyzing discourses. Any act involving sexual harassment turns her from victim to catalyst. Any act can be rewritten by her supervisor as some kind of freakish violation of her mothering role—turning her into a bad, sexually provocative mother. This results in a total removal of any ethical position from which she can lodge a complaint.

The Teacher as Nurturing Mother Figure

One might wonder why the teacher-as-mother discourse has such a powerful role in constituting the subjectivity of elementary teachers. A partial answer is found in historical conditions and how the discourse filtered into the feminization of teaching. Steedman (1985) links the notion of teaching as a kind of mothering to two overlapping historical forces:

> the educative sphere of the middle class mother in the domestic schoolroom of the nineteenth century and from a translation for the educational market of the natural, unforced education that nineteenth century observers saw being imparted by poor (preferably peasant) mothers to their children (p. 151).

The diaries that middle-class women kept on the development of their children reveal the processes and values behind domestic education. For middle-class women such as Elizabeth Cleghorn Gaskell, (Steedman, 1985) mothering had both a moral and an intellectual imperative which she regarded as women's "greatest and highest duties." Middle-class mothers saw themselves as both nurturers and educators concerned with the psychological and the emotional welfare of their children. These descriptions of "good mothering" helped form the unheralded bedrock of modern day psychology and early childhood pedagogy.

While the first source of teaching as mothering comes from middle-class mothers' observations of their children, the second source was based on the naturalistic observations of poor women with theirs. Froebel believed that mothers were educators of their children and that good teaching could be deduced from these methods and made overt. According to Froebel (Herford, 1899), the female teacher must:

> waken and develop in the Human Being every power, every disposition . . . without any Teaching, Reminding or Learning, the true mother does this of herself. But that is not enough: in Addition is needed that being Conscious and acting upon a Creature that is growing Conscious, she do her part Consciously and Consistently, as in Duty bound to guide the Human Being in its regular development (pp. 34–35).

Unlike the intellectual involvement in mothering expressed in the diaries of middle-class women, this pedagogy is "centred on the qualities of instinct, feeling and naturalness" (Steedman, 1985, p. 153). In order to ensure regular development, mothers, nurses, or teachers of children were required to emotionally identify with the child. Due to the prevalence of the cult of the Wordsworthian child in literature as well as the "publicity machine of the Froebelian movement," the public dissemination of his ideas via magazines and books were met with considerable success (Steedman, p. 154).

Hence, there has been a long history of positioning female teachers in very specific ways, all of which contribute to restrictive and prescriptive definitions of good female teacherness. This pedagogy depends on covert authority, as much of what underlies these practices goes unsaid in staff meetings, classrooms, and ministries of education. The invisible, seemingly noncoercive power of naturalized maternal love creates the illusion of freedom on which the child-centered pedagogy depends (Walkerdine, 1990). Since the nurturing capacity of women is so tightly bound up with notions of progressive teaching, is it any wonder that when teachers question the very fictional powers that make modern schooling possible that their queries fall on deaf ears?

Conclusion

The "wedgie" described at the beginning of this chapter was originally seen by the teacher as sexually aggressive behavior performed by "a little bastard." She succumbed to other, less confrontational interpretations due to the cumulative layering of different discourses which manipulate female teachers. These forces coerce teachers into describing events in terms which do not contest the almost religiously guarded innocence of the child. When administrators reinforce the "truth" of these "common sense" notions about the nature of harassment by blaming the teacher, both teachers and students are prevented from seeing the more systemic elements which help shape this form of violence.

School decision makers can be as unresponsive to the diverse needs of their staff as they are to many of their students. Nevertheless, by using poststructural analysis, we can chip away at these supposed truths by opening up a competing discursive space that destabilizes the debilitating effects of these dominant discourses. This may bring about some change which, although it will not "truthfully capture the essence" of the harassment, will allow some further resistance with a theoretical foundation, and thus, provide the basis for a much needed examination of the several issues surrounding acts of elementary student sexual violation.

References

Briskin, L. (1990). *Feminist pedagogy: Teaching and learning liberation*. Feminist Perspectives no.19. Ottawa: CRIAW/ICREF.

Herford, W. H. (1899). *The student's Froebel*. London: Isbister.

Lather, P. (1991). *Getting smart: Feminist research and pedagogy within the postmodern*. New York: Routledge.

Linn, E., Stein, N. D., and Young, J., with S. Davis. (1992) Bitter lessons for all: Sexual harassment in schools. In J. Sears (Ed.), *Sexuality and the curriculum: The policies and practices of sexuality education*. (pp. 106–123). New York: Teachers College.

Luke, Carmen. (1992). Feminist politics in radical pedagogy. In C. Luke and J. Gore (Eds.), *Feminisms and critical pedagogy* (pp. 25–53). New York: Routledge.

Mani, L. (1992). Cultural theory, colonial texts: Reading eyewitness accounts of widow burning. In Grossberg, Nelson, and Theichler (Eds.), *Cultural Studies* (pp. 392–408). New York: Routledge.

Marcus, S. (1992). Fighting bodies, fighting words: A theory and politics of rape prevention. In J. Butler and J. Scott (Eds.), *Feminists theorize the political* (pp. 385–403). New York: Routledge, Chapman & Hall.

Nemni, C. (1992). Sexual harassment: What it is and what it's not. *OPSTF PAR Viewpoint, 8*.

Ontario Human Rights Code, R.S.O. 1990, C.H. 19, s. 7(2) & 7(3).

Riger, S. (1991). Gender dilemmas in sexual harassment policies and procedures. *American Psychologist, 46,* (5), 497–505.

Steedman, C. (1985). The mother made conscious: The historical development of a primary school pedagogy. *History Workshop, 20,* 149–63.

Toronto Board of Education. (1992). *Knowing your rights: Sexual harassment policy*. Toronto: Toronto Board of Education.

Walkerdine, V. (1990). *Schoolgirl fictions*. London: Verso.

Weber, E. (1984). *Ideas influencing early childhood education: A theoretical analysis*. New York: Teachers College.

Weed, E. (1989). *Introduction: Terms of reference. Coming to terms: Feminism, theory, politics*. New York: Routledge.

Chapter 10

Learning in the Learning Place:
Case Studies of Harassment in a
Post-secondary Institution[1]

Catharine E. Warren

Harassment, as defined by the Canadian Human Rights Act, is any discriminatory practice involving behavior ranging from: verbal abuse or threats, unwelcome remarks, unwelcome invitations or requests, condescension or paternalism that undermines self-respect; through unnecessary physical contact; to physical assault. Harassment constitutes behavior with systemic origins. Consequently, harassment can be viewed as resulting in systemic violence as defined in the first chapter.

Continual political action on the part of the women's movement inside and outside of educational institutions has resulted in attention to the issue of sexual harassment at the policy, legal, and administrative levels (Briskin and Coulter, 1992, p. 250). However, this attention does not address administrative harassing behavior. Power dynamics, based on gender, race, and other characteristics, operate in mundane, taken-for-granted and "common-sense" ways (Ng, 1993). These attributes have systemic qualities which go beyond the individual and become embedded as routine operation within the university (p. 193).

When examined from a systemic perspective, harassment can be viewed as more than unwanted behavior by individuals who should know better, or who do know better and persist in that behavior. Harassment can be seen as abuse which is possible whenever there is a differential in power. Bureaucracies, based as they are on power differentials, structurally contain the potential for abuse. Conscious acknowledgment of that potential, along with care not to exploit the potential, is necessary by those occupying leadership positions. Systemic and personal opportunities for harassment dovetail and need to be acknowledged.

Major institutions of patriarchal capitalism such as the family, the church, the workplace, and the school, typically are structured in hierarchical ways which ensure power differences. The structural features of inequity are based on levels of socially designated competency making the execution of harassing behavior possible. The structural proclivity for inequality resides within the hierarchical nature of institutions and the designated roles within that structure. As Ng (1993) reminds us:

> Sexism and racism are systemic in that, routinized in institutions, they have become ways of thinking about and treating groups of people unequally as if these ideas and treatments are "normal"; they are common sense and thus not open to interrogation. These ways of doing things keep certain individuals and groups in dominant and subordinate positions, producing the structural inequality we see both in the education system and in the workplace (p. 195).

This chapter explores, through two case studies, the extent to which harassment may be seen to be an integral part of the postsecondary structure. The first case study in particular gives insights into the extent to which postsecondary institutions depend upon a transference of traditional roles from institutions such as the family and school thus providing role continuance and stability. The case studies illustrate a process through which people who raise questions about the psychopathology of harassment as an appropriate management tool "learn their place" and are silenced.

Circling the Wagons

In the summer of 1988, a first-year graduate class thanked their male instructors by inviting a scantily dressed stripper to the last class. She sat on their laps and fed them chocolates. One instructor was embarrassed but said nothing; the other played into the experience, had his picture taken with her, and later circulated the pictures around the department.

The graduating third-year class was also invited for the surprise and some were offended. Eight women students spoke to Karen, the graduate studies coordinator, about the incident. She advised them to describe the incident in a letter and promised that the incident would be discussed with the program advisory committee. In the letter, the students suggested that the program goals needed to be reviewed.

Karen was angrily confronted by the committee when she circulated copies of the letter to them. The instructors and some others on the committee felt the letter was accusing the two instructors of professional misconduct. Karen discussed the matter with the dean. He also viewed the letter as an attack on the professional conduct of the male instructors and said "Of course, they (the instructors) would fight back!" He assumed that the problem was a personality conflict between Karen and the two instructors and offered to set up a forum in which they could debate the issue. Karen refused to participate because she sensed it would be a gladiatorial event.

When Karen tried to resolve the issue with her two male colleagues they accused her of "inciting" the women and insisted that she should write a letter advising them to retract the letter. When she said that she was unable to do this, she was accused of being unwilling "to cooperate."

Several committee meetings later, the eight women who had signed the original letter were invited to an evening meeting in a university lounge—with refreshments—to try and resolve the issue. Karen asked a male colleague, a specialist in communications and human resource management, to chair the meeting. At the meeting it became apparent that he would not play a neutral role. He arranged the chairs in the lounge with the five male colleagues on one side of a long table and Karen and the eight students on the other. He told them that the purpose of the meeting was to get the writers to rescind their letter and to write another one. The questioning began: What kind of scientific evidence did the writers have for their assertion that the program goals needed to be reviewed? How did they collect their data in order to reach this conclusion? Would they now sign another letter that was less critical of the program?

The women explained that they wrote the letter because they cared about the program, and because the program itself encouraged them to be participatory in their own learning and to critique educational programs. Especially singled out for verbal attack was one woman who was ill and thus the most vulnerable in the group. The other male colleagues looked on with discomfort but did not raise a voice against the process of interrogation. The women refused to retract the original letter.

The next day, a distressed Karen briefed the dean on what had happened. His assessment was that of course the men would behave that way! Their professional competence was being challenged. "What do you want me to do?" he asked. Karen suggested that a letter from someone in a senior position, to each of the women, indicating that what had happened was unfortunate would be appropriate. He refused since that would sound like an apology, which would assign guilt to the instructors.

Karen had no further choices. She told the women that they could take the issue to the sexual harassment committee for review but they decided that to do so would jeopardize their graduation. Shortly afterwards, both of the instructors received administrative promotions.

This case raises many questions. To what extent do unexamined patriarchal assumptions pertaining to male authority affect the quality of leadership in postsecondary education? Are leadership roles based on the unexamined assumptions of those male role templates used in family, church, school, and professional life? Is fear of the erosion of male privilege behind backlash attacks against women who question judgments made by male instructors and administrators? To what extent is the confidence and self-esteem of young women eroded or blocked in its development in our educational institutions by harassing attitudes? Is higher education a positive learning place for women, or is it a place where women "learn their place"? Do women have the right to raise questions about the process of their education and the experiences they are subjected to in the learning place? If so, is harassment the price they must pay for challenging the patriarchal order?

Postsecondary institutions are organized as bureaucracies. Morgan (1986) in a chapter titled "Organizations as Psychic Prisons" noted that this bureaucratic approach fosters rational, analytical, and instrumental characteristics, all associated with the Western stereotype of maleness, while downplaying abilities traditionally viewed as "female," such as intuition, nurturing, and empathic support. Consequently, bureaucracies result in a predisposition for an organizational culture in which men and the women who enter the fray, joust and jostle for positions of dominance like stags contesting the leadership of their herd (Morgan, 1986, p. 211). From such a perspective a bureaucracy can be seen as favoring male dominance in its competency claims.

Furthermore, those working in bureaucratic institutions typically bring to their roles experiences of other institutions such as the family and the school. Morgan states that "the dominant influence of the male is rooted in the hierarchical relations found in the patriarchal family which . . . serves as a factory for authoritarian ideologies" (1986, p. 211). Included in those experiences in the family is often a template or model of "the male as head of household" and the privilege that goes along with the head-of-household position. Both men and women may bear this template of male-dominated family structures, resulting in feelings of impotence accompanied by fear and a dependence on authority; this has psychic consequences for those enacting roles in organizational settings (Morgan, 1986, p. 12). Ng (1993), too, notes that educational institutions reflect such patriarchal forms of dominance and control in their practices (p. 250).

Thus "success" in post-secondary institutions requires merging the experience of patriarchal privilege brought from other institutional experiences with the bureaucratic competency role expectation whose structure may already give an edge to traditional maleness. The merger can have surprising consequences. For example, a woman faculty member who supported a graduate student in her appeal, heard a male department head tell the appeal committee that the faculty woman should be "punished" for her accusations of bias. If a male faculty member had broken rank and supported a student would the comment have been the same?

In post-secondary institutions it is sometimes assumed that competency and patriarchal privilege are one and the same. From such a perspective, challenges to that merged privilege/competency template are not viewed as legitimate. Bureaucratic authority based on levels of competency can be maintained only if there is consensus that competency occurs not only in the decisions made but increasingly in the process by which those judgments are made. Otherwise, challenges to the legitimacy claims of the competency-based position will continue to be raised.

Cohen (1987), in his view of structuration theory, contends that we have a fair degree of freedom to act despite being locked into a social structure such as a bureaucracy. He argues that there is a dialectic of control involving the asymmetrical access to resources through which people can influence the behaviors of others. The contention of this chapter is that those with administrative responsibilities can be open to forms of influence and management styles other than harassment. However, senior administrators can create a climate that legitimates and models a range of harassing behaviors which, in turn, negate the possibility of alternative positive forms.

The following case demonstrates how many individuals (both male and female) within post-secondary institutions depend on harassment for the maintenance of their position of authority. Men, and in this case also a woman in an authoritative position, carry the patriarchal template in their heads and use the force of harassment to ensure the maintenance of their authority.

Closing Ranks

In 1990, the atmosphere in the department of a post-secondary institution could be described as sullied and poisoned after just three months with a new head. The support staff complained that the new department head was "a womanizer." One married woman reported discreetly to colleagues that he had called her at home and invited her to dinner (alone); another woman left her job quickly after telling coworkers that he had propositioned her. A new untenured faculty member jogged regularly with the head for several months until he asked her out for dinner and a movie while his wife was out of town. She declined. The head seldom saw her after that but became increasingly critical about her work and she took a new position elsewhere within the year. There were other instances. Some support staff took stress leave. Meanwhile, staff and faculty grew increasingly afraid to speak to others for fear of repercussions.

One day it became known that, in his private life, the head had been convicted of a criminal harassment offense. Faculty members asked two top administrators to discuss the implications of the conviction. One of the senior administrators responded: "Is this conviction true? Have you checked it out?" The faculty members later found out that, once the conviction became known, the head approached this administrator with an offer to resign. His offer had been refused.

Damage control began. The faculty members were told that the head's behavior must be "one of the best kept secrets on the campus." Each person in the department was interviewed by one of the senior administrators. At a public meeting, the entire department of academics and support staff were told by the senior administration that they had been imagining the worst of the new head and that the problem was based on their gossiping. In private, the faculty members were assured that the head would "get help" so that he would become a better administrator. He continued to the end of his four-year term.

An "old boys' network" was operating. There was a public downplaying of the importance of the criminal conviction and a public chastisement of those who felt they had been abused. There was a stonewalling of reports by women who complained even though they understood that their concerns regarding the inappropriate behavior of the head probably would not fit the present sexual harassment guidelines of the institution. The process of investigation turned out to be a most dispiriting one devoid of judicial guidelines. As a consequence, support staff, women faculty, and those men who spoke up about the behavior, learned from the experience that administrative harassment was not confined to the lower echelons of a bureaucracy but seemed to be indigenous to the entire structure of the institution. The "leadership" for the administrative harassment came from the top of the organization; it was not just an aberrant part of the whole.

Conclusion

These two cases are cold examples of the "chilly climate" as first described by Hall and Sandler (1982). Systemic violence affects not only faculty and students but support staff as well. There is a notable absence of a discourse which could dissect or deconstruct the reasons why these cases could not be viewed seriously as administrative harassment and why the prevailing climates of post-secondary institutions remain relatively unexamined. In the meantime, the poisoned and chilly climate takes its toll with stress-related illness and nonproductivity. This climate has serious implications for learning in these "learning places."

What is the true nature of the learning which the situations described here teach? All of us, as faculty, students, and staff, learn that the voices of women usually count less. For women to raise their voices means they must be silenced through swift deprecating action made possible through the unchallenged power of the bureaucracy. Systemic violence thus successfully inoculates psyches for another generation of acceptance of harassment.

Note

1. An earlier version of this chapter was presented to the Canadian Association for the Study of Women and Education as part of the Canadian Society for the Study of Education Conference in Montreal, Quebec, Canada, June 1995.

References

Briskin, L. and Coulter, R. (1992). Feminist pedagogy: Challenging the normative. *Canadian Journal of Education, 17*(3), 247–63.

Cohen, I. (1987). Structuration theory. In A. Giddens and J. Turner (Eds.), *Social theory today* (pp. 273–308). Stanford: Stanford University Press.

Hall, R. and Sandler, B. (1982). *The classroom climate: A chilly one for women*? Washington: Project on the Status and Education of Women, Association of American Colleges.

Morgan, G. (1986). *Images of organization*. Beverley Hills, CA: Sage.

Ng, R. (1993). "A Woman out of control": Deconstructing sexism and racism in the university. *Canadian Journal of Education, 18* (13), 189–205.

Chapter 11

Systemic Violence:
Linking Women's Stories,
Education, and Abuse[1]

Laura Ho, Kathie Webb & Anne Hughson

So long as men and women inhabit the same society and live overlapping lives, each sex will be affected by the education of the
other. Unenlightened policies of female education will inevitably
redound on males (Jane Roland Martin, 1985, p. 5).

Violence in society and in education is often construed in
purely physical terms, yet there are far more subtle forms of violence that are just as hurtful, silencing, and damaging. Without
denying that physical violence is damaging both to the individual
and to the broader society, we wish to draw attention to the violence to a person's identity that occurs when personal experience
and meaning are denied by education. Systemic violence is covert
yet pervasive throughout education. It is not necessarily intentional, but insidiously exerts a degenerative effect on the social
whole. It is impossible to point a finger and lay blame against any
single perpetrator, or to create a policy to eliminate it. In our conversations we will speak to the "systemic violence" of abuse perpetrated through policies, practices, and structures in educational
and social systems. We question the kind of education that silences
the stories of girls and women and consider what this means for all
students.

Though we conduct research in diverse fields, we have been
drawn together by common questions such as Gaskell, McLaren
and Novrogodsky's (1989) question: "What is worth knowing?"

160

Each of us, through our work with immigrants, with women and girls in education, with women who have experienced sexual and physical abuse, and through our own experiences, has encountered cultural and educational practices that deny personal stories and experiences. Two questions we raise for discussion are: "Why is it that education silences women's stories?" and, "Why are our lives not seen as part of our learning?"

Our experiences, and the experiences of those whose stories we retell, are quite different. However, the common thread of abuse, systemic abuse, by educational and social systems links them. We have chosen to tell our stories as individuals within the context of this narrative. The personal pronoun will be used to reflect the fact that this chapter is a combination of several stories told by several voices. We are bringing our stories together in order to call for a pedagogical shift on two fronts: valuing human experience, and recognition of knowledge as socially constructed. Such a perspective would value not only the stories of girls and women, but the personal knowledge of all students. We are asking for the reconstruction of curriculum from this perspective.

Depersonalized: Experiences of Immigrant Women
(Laura Ho)

The experience of immigrant women with the systems of their adopted communities provides a powerful focus for the politics of difference. Here, at a point where differing cultural expectations, histories, languages, races, and social understandings interact, it is possible to encounter the lived consequences of violent racist acts. These acts are sometimes committed knowingly, but more often are not. Regardless of intent, however, outcomes are similar since the individuals are treated as essentially "other," as not meriting the understanding or consideration shown more culturally knowable students. I will refer to the adult education system specifically because that is where I became a witness to the violence of unchallenged pledges of "community," "capacity," and "opportunity."

The word "systemic" derives, according to *The Concise Oxford Dictionary*, from its application to physiological systems. As compared with the word "systematic," which describes a methodical or planned activity, system is applied to the function of "the bodily system as a whole not confined to a particular part" (Concise Oxford Dictionary, 1972, p. 1085). In our context, systemic proves to be a very apt word because it focuses attention on the problem of systemic health, and brings into question the effect of aspects of the corpus on the hypothetical whole: the community. Young (1990) talks about the problem of systems with reference to the term "community," arguing that such an ideal "denies difference in the sense of the contradictions and ambiguities of social life." Young argues for a politics of difference as an alternative to the sometimes oppressive notion of community, a politics allowing for the recognition and affirmation of groups, a celebration of distinctive cultures.

Similarly, Gaskell et al. (1989) denounce the treatment of experiential difference, whether it concerns women or minorities, as deficit, and draw our attention instead to the possibility of "a politics of opportunity." In both instances, writers have suggested that it is the "generic approach" to the construction of the social and political which requires adaptation in order to unlock the varying talents and ambitions of all people. I will introduce two immigrant women in Canadian adult education and highlight institutional strategies which contributed to their experience of violence at school.

Immigrant women may initially enter the adult education context because of language or educational difference. Their use of their mother tongue or of a dialect of English identifies them as differing from the community, thus impairing their ability to compete economically. For government and people within the receiving society generally, an unfamiliar language becomes a symbol of difference to be eradicated. For Canadians, insistence upon immigrants' quick, efficient mastery of English or French has become a vehicle of depersonalization, a means for diverting our attention away from individual differences among immigrant men and women. This monolithic preoccupation with annihilating language differences has had the effect of obscuring the history, competence, and aspirations of such women and has contributed to the construction of an abstracted and unchallenged notion of what is needed by immigrants to achieve participation in Canadian society. Whether the presumed benefits of English-language study are borne out in women's experience, however, is never examined. The character of the broader language environment, the existence of a range of languages in the broader society remains an issue unaddressed within the system of adult education. The plurality of languages spoken of by Caputo (1988, p. 69) is silent in the mainstream of adult education.

The annihilation of the person in the push for language training has serious consequences for individuals. An Iranian woman, offers her feelings about studying English and being locked out of the world.

Azar

> I feel not happy. I'm very quiet now, you know. Inside my body is very sad because I don't . . . I can't say anything and I can't talk. Most of the time I feel that learning English is like being in jail (Azar cited in Ho, 1993, p. 93).

For Azar, and many like her, learning English has not resulted in an opening of doors. A poet and a politically aware woman in her native Iran, she now depends on the reports of English-speaking friends to keep up with events in her home country. Her need to make sense of the discontinuity of her life has been completely overlooked by her teachers. There is no space for her language or her wealth of experience in many of the programs available to her.

Azar continues to struggle for a place within a Canada which has been and continues to be, by its tradition of immigration, constantly reinterpreted and reinvented. Azar, too, is reinventing Canada beyond the structures of programs established for the benefit of the community. Initial attempts to negotiate a meaningful place in her own education, however, have met with unanticipated results. Even though Azar is a woman who has learned to assert her views in limited English, she found her participation unheeded. Azar speaks about her experience with her teacher and the administration at a local college:

> "She [the teacher] told us the government said to read the newspaper. For five months we had newspaper. I didn't learn any words."

"What about the boss?' I asked. "Did you complain to the boss of the college about the teacher, then?"

Yes, she had tried: "The first time, ten students went together to talk with the boss, and he didn't listen. He said you are students for just five months, and then that's it. If you want to change, you can study more after this five months. It's right now or nothing!"

Azar was studying in a program which received federal government sponsorship. The administrator was right: If she left, she would get nothing. From Azar's perspective (and clearly from that of others) the program was irrelevant. Azar's challenge was quickly dismissed because she was deemed irrelevant to the broader system in which she sought participation. She lacked the social power to be heard by the institution (Weedon, 1987, p. 111).

Azar's views may have been outrightly dismissed by her school, but her experience does not reflect the even more insidious kind of institutional violence suffered by Amy.

Amy

Amy was a very willing student, a new immigrant from Hong Kong. After the failure of her family's business, Amy realized that she would have to make a career change and look for a job. She would not be able to work in business or as a teacher, even though she had studied and worked in education in Hong Kong for many years. She did not know what kind of career would best suit her in this country.

Amy tells how she became involved in training for office work. She chose office work because she couldn't carry heavy loads. When asked what kind of counseling she had, she said:

Oh, in the program they helped me, but the problem is I don't mind to do any job. It means that I can work in many fields. The problem is so it's not good for me. I can change jobs easily. Just like my friend, she only want to be an accounting clerk. That's all. Others she does not want.

"But," I persisted, "you can get into lots of things that pay very poorly and maybe aren't suitable for you, even though they aren't heavy work. What kind of help did you get in terms of knowing how much money people make and what the opportunities are?" Amy had not thought about this and no one had offered her any help with this kind of planning as a part of her course—a course called Effective Career Planning for Immigrants.

Several points need to be made concerning Amy's story. Amy is resigned to never working again in education. She understands too well the tacit message of the Canadian system, namely, that her foreign qualifications mean that it is unlikely she will be able to work as a teacher. But what about related fields? Amy did not receive any counseling which even considered her professional background. Instead, her statement that she would try anything was likely interpreted as meaning that any kind of training would do. Amy trusted that the counselor would do his/her best to help her make decisions. An explicit goal for the counselor, based on funding to provide Employment Training, was to get clients into something, anything, as a consequence of the course. It seems that program success, that is, finding immediate solutions for clients, is more important than finding meaningful outcomes for individual students.

Amy seems a willing accomplice in her own victimization. Her cultural expectation, that others will do their best to help, betrays her. Azar, in comparison, expresses a clear understanding of her place or lack of place within the adult education system. Yet a question remains about the more powerful participants in this relationship. What has the adult education system done for either of these two women? Azar has lost the context of her poetry; Amy has lost her education and career. Very few people in Canada will ever have the opportunity to meet and get to know either woman as the accomplished persons they are. Their teachers have never known and, in all likelihood, will never know them.

Resisting Conformity That Denies Self (Kathie Webb)

"Systemic violence" emerged in my doctoral research in both my observations and experiences. I spent eight months in a classroom as a researcher and coteacher. Here I met a grade seven student named "Mary Jane." I recognized, in Mary Jane, a similar struggle to the one I was experiencing as a female graduate student in male-dominated graduate classes in staff development and educational administration. One of the connections was Mary Jane's resistance to a school policy (which required conforming behavior on her part) and my resistance to a required view of education (as hierarchically organized) in my graduate coursework.

I question educational policies and practices which silence the stories of girls and women and examine the negative effects of the label "bad girl" that is applied to women and girls who resist policies and practices which impose conformity: conformity which women and girls recognize as denying self—as denying what they know. A part of this analysis focuses on how this repression, this violence, affects all students. My analysis begins with an example of a repressive administrative system intended to control student behavior.

Mary Jane

The administration at Mary Jane's school implemented a policy called DAAM sheets (Daily Activity and Attendance Monitoring) which required each teacher to award a point (+2, +1, 0, −1, or −2) for cooperative behavior to each student for every period of every day of every week. The scores for each student were totaled daily and published weekly. Students with positive scores were told they were "good" students, students with negative scores were told they were "bad" students. At the beginning and end of each day, the "bad" students' names were called over the intercom ordering them to the principal's office. One of the effects of this policy was that for girls (and boys), behavior was being confused with academic performance and potential; that is, bad behavior was being interpreted as "bad" student (Webb, 1994).

In 1992, Mary Jane was a grade seven student and the leader of a small cohort of girls in her grade. With a constant minus score she excelled at the school level as the "bad girl." The teacher felt Mary Jane had a lot more talent than she allowed her teachers to see because she chose not to achieve in areas she deemed meaningless. Encouraged to express her ideas and experiences in writing, she wrote some outstanding poetry indicating her academic potential. The teacher believed Mary Jane's maturity, possibly due to her experiences out of school, had worked against her: "Mary Jane sees the hypocrisy in a system that claims it is about academics, and yet a student can be put out of class for wearing a hat or the wrong kind of coat." Halfway through grade eight Mary Jane began skipping school on Fridays. She plans to leave school at the end of the year because she hates it so much.

Mary Jane's success at being a bad girl reminds me of Signithia Fordham's (1993) "loud black girls." Mary Jane's resistance is a stance—a choice not to achieve. The sense of threat to self in conforming to the school code of student behavior seems evident—conforming would deny her sense of self. My concern is similar to Fordham's, in that I ask, "At what cost is she succeeding in being a bad girl?" Will there be a point at which she is able to step out of this performance or is she doomed to live out this story indefinitely? Will she and her friends, the other bad girls, come to accept and believe they are "less than" others because of the response to them by the teachers and administrators? She was very successful in her defiance, in that most of her teachers left her alone and did not try to help her. She was allowed to do badly at school. Her most frequent punishment was to be removed from class or suspended from school for days at a time. This practice worked to prevent her from getting full access to her teachers and from the opportunity to learn. Fordham's question echoes in my head: How do you survive if you are marginalized?

My own story is not dissimilar to Mary Jane's in that it also makes problematic the conditions under which women learn. In my sixteenth year of teaching in Australia, and after seven years as a department head in a large high school, I enrolled in coursework for a Master of Education degree hoping to explore further the ways in which collaborative relationships work for teacher development and for problem solving. In courses entitled "Staff Development i and ii," I was required to complete assignments on "task analysis" using military handbooks. The philosophy of "training" was all too pervasive in the management orientation which provided the framework for teacher development in these courses.

I puzzled at, and struggled with, the gap between my personal experience and the ideas that I was required to learn—and advocate if I was to "achieve" in these courses. Not able to frame my dilemma in epistemological terms, I kept wondering and waiting until what I "knew" about teacher development would be validated at the academy. It didn't happen. Still seeking affirmation of my personal knowledge, I commenced doctoral studies, convinced that a Ph.D. would provide the opportunity to explore what I knew and how I had come to know.

I was bitterly disappointed to find that even at the doctoral level I was expected to be subordinate in intelligence, contribution, and performance to my male counterparts. I identify (I use the present tense, because at the time I still could not name the abuse I was experiencing) with Lewis's (1986) experience of being silenced in graduate classrooms by men who verbally took up all the space. The dynamics of graduate classrooms disturbed me greatly. I did not understand why the personal was often treated as irrelevant. I felt frustrated and left out in courses where the curriculum, teaching strategies, assignments, and mode of assessment had been designed by the professor. I felt irritated and offended by classroom strategies concerned more with regurgitating the content of textbooks than with engaging students in consciousness-raising discussions. The discourse of outcomes, product, measurement, targets, mandated policies, and unproblematized top-down power relations was in conflict with how I had worked collaboratively with teachers for mutual development for more than ten years.

I found it painful to have my ideas dismissed by fellow students who took comfort in the status quo for hierarchical organizations and who reveled in management theories adapted from the world of business. The comment, "You don't know what you are talking about!" tells of the superior attitude of students who subscribed to the dominant ideology for schooling and the disparagement with which they treated any other graduate student who chose to think differently. The comment of one professor (made frequently as a response to stories told by women students) is revealing of the profound ways in which women were silenced. After sharing a personal story in which I tried to make connections between my experience in schools and the topic at hand, the professor's dismissive comment, "Now let's get back on track," was a clear message to all present that my story (and other women's stories) were irrelevant to our studies.

In resisting and in attempting to construct my own curriculum, in attempting to claim my own status as a knowledge creator at a graduate level, I met with confrontation from both students (mainly male) and certain professors (male) with a vested interest in maintaining the status quo. In graduate classrooms, I also experienced the double bind (Lewis, 1992) of needing to speak (to share my perceptions) and to remain silent (for fear of reprisal from both students and professor). I experienced the discourse of most of my graduate classrooms as politically oriented towards objectivity, management theories, and standardization. It was, and largely remains, a discourse which excludes my experiences of education.

That I have survived these negative experiences and have continued with graduate studies is due in large measure to the encouragement of a supportive and caring doctoral advisory committee and a supportive community of graduate students. My determination to make sense of my own experience and my resistance to what I now name as a violent and abusive education has not been without cost. I wonder how many women (and men) do not survive the violence. I wonder who leaves the academy in order to retain a sense of self.

Devaluation: Violence from an Intimate Partner
(Ann Hughson)

The "private matter" of women who are beaten by their intimate partners has only recently been of public interest. Currently there is a public agenda to provide a social response to this problem by building safe places to which women may flee. The professional staffing and public funding of such shelters have not reduced the enormity of the problem. There is still little understanding of what it would take to ensure that women and their children are safe in their homes and in their communities. It is also possible that when we frame the problem as one of having safe places for women to escape to, so much goes unanswered/unexplored. The separation of women into shelters may silence them and thus influence how we as a society think about women and violence.

Feminist theories have examined the nature of oppressive social arrangements based on sex, race, and class and have critiqued
the central organizing principle for much of Western thought,
which lies in the nature of a set of oppositional dualisms.
Dualisms—either/or, you/me, good/bad, high/low—are so deeply
embedded in Western knowledge structures that they often seem
like natural categories. This assumption of dualism generally includes a hierarchical relationship between the terms, valuing one
and devaluing the other (white and black; light and dark). Such assumptions, built into language and unspoken cultural agreements
about "the good" or "the real," have the result of naturalizing social
inequities to make them appear unchangeable or inevitable.

Women as a class or group have been, throughout Western
history, associated with the devalued characteristics in such pairs.
The primary dualisms of Western thought particularly instrumental in legitimizing women's subordination, are those between reason and emotion, private and public, nature and culture, subject
and object, and mind and body. Each pair conceptually relegates
women to peripheral, secondary, or inferior status (Rakow, 1992).

It is from this interpretation of dualism, as a systematic, organizing principle that places women in an inferior position, that I
offer the research that I am engaged in as part of a discussion of systemic violence. This discussion is about the danger of oppositional
dualism—devaluation. The radical feminist treatment of the dualism of culture and nature offers a central thesis: that men's treatment of women and nature is violent (Daly, 1984; Dvorkin, 1974).

Academics, human service professionals, and social activists
have taken an interest in the topic of wife abuse and made it a public agenda. The typical nonpolitical stance of the researcher or
helping professional has led to a diagnosis of the problem in medical or psychiatric terms and an offer to "fix" the woman on the
basis of this framework (assess, diagnose, treat) while ignoring the
political and social context (Walker, 1979). Meanwhile activist
women have worked hard to protect battered women while trying
to change the social and political environment (Hoff, 1990). Each
approach has been criticized. The professional, in her eagerness to
fix, diagnoses the woman and ignores the social influences, and the
activist, in her passion for cultural change, ignores the objective
search for knowledge.

Acknowledging this tension about the nature of "the problem" of wife abuse, I have attempted to step aside from this debate by having conversations with women who have "known" violence in a very personal way. It is a way of creating the space in which to tell our stories. As Susan Heald (1994) has said, "If we have no place to tell our story publicly, then privately, we lie to ourselves."

The notion that different people go through different experiences and thus gain widely varying understandings of what constitutes reality or truth results in the "inescapable contextuality of knowledge." It is impossible to find one objective truth upon which all would agree. Relocating questions about knowledge and truth to positions within the conversations of humankind does seem to break the bondage of objective detachment and create a forum for cooperative debate about our knowledge about everyday, practical life. So this work has chosen a process that Rorty (1989) describes as "continuing conversation rather than discovering truth," by talking with women who have had a personal and devastating experience with violence at the hands of a husband who said that he loved her.

Activists have long critiqued the naturalness, inevitability, and presumed benefits of marriage. Victims of emotional and physical violence know that marriage is not the safe haven for women that the patriarchal ideology espouses, yet the pervasive cultural influences that maintain oppressive social arrangements based on sex, race and class often lead researchers to ask questions that blame the battered women: "Why does she stay?" or worse, "What did she do to set it off?" Other questions, questions that ask women what it means to feel safe, why it is risky for them to live in their homes, and when do they "know" they will not get hurt, what can hurt them, when do they know that they must flee, and why must they flee. These questions suggest useful alternative questions that could help in gaining knowledge.

Our life is our education. Three women, all mothers between the ages of thirty and fifty, agreed to tell their stories and to reflect on their meaning. Each women told a different story of what led her to know that she could only be safe if there was a man who would marry her and thus protect her from harm. She was not told what might hurt her but rather, that she must learn what a good girl must do to be safe. "Good" meant acting and talking in certain ways that did not challenge her position as inferior to boys. "Bad" meant being too loud, too competitive, too independent, not saving herself for the man who would love her, not remembering that she may not be safe alone.

Each woman clearly remembered the important and powerful messages they were given as young girls: "Good girls get married and live happily ever after. . . . Don't worry, you don't need to be that smart in school, it's too hard . . . Don't worry if you didn't win or you weren't the best at that, it is not important. . . . When you get married you won't have to worry about those other things." Each woman described clear messages delivered by mothers, fathers, brothers, teachers, and other older adults that said she would be at risk unless she "had" a man to protect her and she should invest her time, energy, intellect, creativity, and resources in finding one and making "it" work. The "truths" that we grew up with about "good" and "bad", sent messages that said "good" girls will seek protection from men, and it was "bad" to think that you could look after yourself or be interested in pursuing things other than a man. For one woman, these messages were being given throughout her childhood while at the same time she witnessed her mother being physically and emotionally abused by her father. One women reflected on how she came to believe that:

> When I was locked in the apartment, ridiculed in front of others, abandoned when I found out I was pregnant, hurt, it was because I had been "bad." I just didn't get him to love me enough, I had to do more to be loved. . . . I would be safe if I could figure out what I was doing wrong.

The stories of these women allowed us to talk about what was safe to tell, what was safe to know, what was safe to do, what was safe to feel. One woman described the only safe way to think, feel, know, act: "When I could be alone in my room listening to my music and no one else would know what I was thinking or feeling. No one could touch me." One woman talked about what the risks were if she did something that was not safe: "I would be laughed at, abandoned, physically hurt, controlled until I obeyed, told I was stupid, and often my mother said, 'Don't get carried away'." In this project, there are many pieces to explore. Each woman talks now from a place where she describes herself as safer and that place is not outside of her but within her.

Analysis: Connections within Stories
(Ho, Webb, and Hughson)

While the social and cultural rhetoric of the western world is that women are valued and cared for by men, large numbers of women are physically and sexually abused by men. A similar paradox exists in the educational rhetoric that "education is good for you" when many policies and practices act systemically to violate the person and the personal. Negative experiences and systemic abuse are not limited to women and girls. What we know of women's experiences can advance more caring practices and responses to violence in education and society which will benefit men and women, girls and boys. "We are commonly told that schools are places of emancipation, but in fact schools were historically created not to make that possibility real. Schools were put into place to control social and political action" (Lewis, 1995, personal communication).

The contradiction implicit in the safety promised through marriage was apparent in the stories told by each of the women. Their experiences are similar to those of Anne-Louise Brookes:

> Throughout my many years of schooling, apart from the work I did in a feminist context, I encountered not one teacher who taught me to critique the relations of power which enable men to violate women. . . . Not one adult taught me that women are not necessarily safe in their own homes. Instead, I was taught the illusion that I would be cared for, and protected, by men (Brookes, 1992, p. 130).

Brookes (1992) criticizes her schooling because she was not taught that ideology is a concept. She says women and men are taught to accept the ideology of social inequality, albeit in different ways, and hence find it difficult to critique the illusions "which work like truth when one is not taught to critique them." (p. 130) She suggests that the concepts of femininity and masculinity, and the ways these are constructed, need to be critiqued in school along with the disproportionate power and social relations that exist between men and women.

The Meaning/s of Violence and the Control of Meaning

The violence perpetrated against women and girls needs to be understood in terms of annihilation of the person—the damage to self and beliefs about self that result from systemic abuse and abuse by intimate others. When the stories of women and girls are ignored or trivialized in social and educational settings, personal knowledge is violated. Lewis (1993), describes the pain of exclusion from discourse and "invisibility" in graduate classrooms:

> While the experience of being consciously, deliberately and overtly dismissed is painful, the experience of being invisible is brutalizing. To have had our ideas, work, and talent considered and contested might have challenged our critical sense; to have them not even noted denied our existence in the most profound way (Lewis, 1993, p. 137).

Lewis views the violation of women's stories at the academy not as accidental or due to ignorance, but rather as a result of patriarchal control of meaning. Personal knowledge is powerful and it is precisely because of the power of the personal that women's lived realities have been set outside the boundaries of what counts as knowledge. The blinders of "objectivity" and the restrictive codes that forbid personal discourse are required if work is to be considered "academic." This situation has arisen through women's exclusion from theory formation. Women have been denied the status of meaning makers: what counts as common sense is not an arbitrary matter, but a matter of power (Lewis, 1993; Code, 1991).

The serious consequences of the annihilation of the person are further demonstrated in the depersonalization of immigrant women. When Lewis (1993) calls attention to the ways women resist oppression, she examines women's silence as oppression and as an act of resistance. Azar's resistance when she complained to the administrator was useless. The students were treated as receivers of education and not recognized as constructors of knowledge or as having any knowledge or experience worthy of inclusion in the course. Azar's knowledge and experience largely shaped her definition of self, and hence, she felt that she was not valued.

Amy's story also depicts her as a willing accomplice in her own victimization. She does not resist or complain when she is given no counseling. Her trust in her counselor is not only misplaced, but grounded in her own cultural expectations that professionals will do their best to help her. While Amy's failure to criticize those in authority over her can be attributed to the norms of the culture, Amy cannot be blamed for expecting good advice from someone paid to do just that. In both cases, education is abusive because the person who is the student is denied and betrayed.

The Implications of "Systemic Violence" in Education

Education could be used to problematize patriarchal relations of power and authority. Immigrant women, women who have survived sexual and physical abuse by their partners, junior high students, and woman graduate students all experience the debilitating effect of abuse and the affects of "systemic violence" on women and girls' sense of self and how they perceive themselves in relation to their own knowing. Brookes (1992) argues not that women learn differently from men or need a different kind of education, but that their experiences and their knowing need to be included and honored in their education. Brookes' abuse disturbed her identity as a producer of knowledge. Social and educational practices silenced her as a victim of abuse. This silencing made her knowledge invisible and she came to be separate from what she knew. This made it difficult for her to know herself or to imagine herself as the creator of her own knowledge.

Our research stories and Brookes' research challenge education to change practices and policies. Those working in the educational context could respond to systemic violence of women and girls in ways which were meaningful to and would include the voices of those who have experienced abuse. Educational policies in the western world could meet their claims that critical thinking and creative approaches to problem solving are being encouraged for all students. The practices which posit women and girls as received knowers (Belenky et al., 1986) rather than as constructed knowers could be addressed.

The issue of women's safety also has profound social and educational implications. The way women are separated from families and offered shelters is indicative of the way we as a society think about violence. The women described their constructions of what it meant to be safe—even if it meant escaping into their minds to protect themselves. The abuse could be addressed by redirecting the focus and reframing questions about violence. More appropriate questions would be concerned with what happens and how knowledge can be used to change things in the future, rather than a primary focus on blame.

The same issues and questions are at play when we begin to unpack Mary Jane's grade seven experience. The school's response to Mary Jane was to question her behavior and posit it as inappropriate. The policy which mandated point scoring of system-devised appropriate behaviors for students, and the ways that the meanings of the resultant labels of "good student" and "bad student" became embodied with behavior rather than academic performance, remains unquestioned at the school or within the school system that encourages such policies.

The "generic approach" to the construction of the social and political requires adaptation in order to unlock the varying talents and ambitions of all people. Meaningful curriculum cannot be determined externally to students (or to the teacher, as is the case with mandated curriculum). Who decides curriculum is a question relevant at all levels of education and of concern for the education of all students. Language is the "place where actual and possible forms of social organization and their likely social and political consequences are defined and contested" (Weedon, 1987, p. 21). It is certainly no coincidence that language, among all other differences which distinguish Canadian from foreign-born, is a primary focus in Canadian strategies to "provide" education to adult immigrants.

But even a literate white woman with three degrees can experience difficulty and reprisal in attempting to claim an education (Rich, 1979; Gaskell et al., 1989) and establish an identity as a producer of knowledge (Brookes, 1992). There are similarities in the negative responses to women's and girls' resistance to oppressive policies and practices. There are pedagogical implications for understanding the resistance and a need to understand what it means to be educated against self (Noddings, 1984; Lewis, 1993).

The enactment of violence is complex and dynamic—systemic, educationally and socially in the western world. As educational researchers, as academic women, as teachers, and as humanitarians we can consider the ways the sociopolitical construction of violence may be moved along. The challenge is to explore the social effect of violence. Our stories, told from three different but connected perspectives of systemic violence, highlight the contradictions between western societal rhetoric concerning the care and treatment of women and the reality of the abusive experiences of women and girls in educational contexts and in their lives. In linking women's stories, education, and abuse, we are calling for responses to violence that will include and not deny the stories and experiences of women and girls. The development of pedagogies and curricula must include all students and honor the knowledge they bring to the classroom.

Note

1. An earlier version of this chapter was presented to the Canadian Association for the Study of Women and Education as part of the Canadian Society for the Study of Education Conference in Calgary, Alberta, Canada, June 1994.

References

Belenky, M., Clinchy, B., Goldberger, N. and Tarule, J. (1986). *Women's ways of knowing: The development of self, voice and mind.* New York: Basic Books.

Brookes, A. L. (1992). *Feminist pedagogy: An autobiographical approach.* Halifax: Fernwood Publishing.

178 Laura Ho, et al.

Caputo, J. (1988). Beyond aestheticism: Derrida's responsible anarchy. *Research in Phenomenology*, *18*, 59–73.

Code, L. (1991). *What can she know?: Feminist theory and the construction of knowledge*. Ithaca, NY: Cornell University Press.

Concise Oxford Dictionary. (1972). Oxford: Oxford University Press.

Daly, M. (1984). *Pure lust: Elemental feminist philosophy*. Boston: Beacon.

Dvorkin, A. (1974). *Women hating*. New York: Dutton.

Fordham, S. (1993). Those loud black girls: (Black) women, silence, and gender "passing" in the academy. *Anthropology and Education Quarterly*, *24* (1), 3–32.

Gaskell, J., McLaren, A., and Novrogodsky, M. (1989). *Claiming an education: Feminism and Canadian schools*. Toronto: Our Schools/Our Selves Education Foundation.

Heald, S. (1994, June). *Progressivism, paternalism and pathologisation: Possibilities for feminist pedagogy in the university of the 1990s*. Paper presented at the Canadian Women's Studies Association Conference, Calgary, Alberta, Canada.

Ho, L. (1993). *Listening and speaking: Immigrant views of adult education in Edmonton*. Unpublished doctoral dissertation. Edmonton, AB: University of Alberta.

Hoff, L. A. (1990). *Battered women as survivors*. New York: Routledge.

Lewis, M. and Simon, R. (1986). A discourse not intended for her: Learning and teaching within patriarchy. *Harvard Educational Review*, *56* (4), 457–472.

Lewis, M. (1992). Interrupting patriarchy: Politics, resistance and transformation in the feminist classroom. In C. Luke and J. Gore (Eds.), *Feminisms and critical pedagogy* (pp. 167–91). New York: Routledge.

Lewis, M. G. (1993). *Without a word: Teaching beyond women's silences*. New York: Routledge.

Martin, J. R. (1985). *Reclaiming a conversation: The ideal of the educated woman*. New Haven: Yale University Press.

Noddings, N. (1984). *Caring: A feminine approach to ethics and moral education*. Berkeley, CA: University of California Press.

Rakow, L. F. (Ed.) (1992). *Women making meaning*. New York: Routledge.

Rich, A. (1979). *On lies, secrets and silence*. New York: W. W. Norton.

Rorty, R. (1989). *Contingency, irony and solidarity*. New York: Cambridge University Press.

Walker, L (1979). *The battered woman*. New York: Harper Row.

Webb, K. M. (1994, October). *Bad girls: negative labelling of women and girls who resist repressive policies and practices ("systemic violence") in education*. Paper presented at Understanding Self, Understanding Others, 20th Annual Conference Research on Women and Education, St. Paul, MN.

Weedon, C. (1987). *Feminist practice and poststructuralist theory*. Cambridge, MA: Blackwell.

Young, I. M. (1990). The ideal of community and the politics of difference. In L. J. Nicholson (Ed.) *Feminism/ postmodernism*. New York: Routledge.

Part IV

Keeping Promise

Chapter 12

Personal Reconstruction:
When Systemic Violence Stops

———

Myrna Yuzicapi

"Bush nigger, bush nigger, bush nigger," their unisoned voices were cruel as they taunted me. Then they ran away laughing, leaving my lunch strewn about my feet, my new lunch box trampled beyond repair and my new dress torn and dirty. My first day of school. Not ten minutes before, I had been a bright, precocious five-year-old eagerly anticipating the wonder and adventure of going to school. So this is what school is. The teacher said nothing about what had happened. The day progressed and we settled into our phonics, our readers, and set out to be educated.

After school, I asked my mother what "nigger" was. I understood the bush part. When she told me what it meant, I was totally confused. I had seen only one black person in my life, and I had been terrified of him. I believed he was the "bogey man" who would "get me" if I disobeyed. My world no longer made sense.

Ours was the only native family in the area. I was the eldest in the family, and so was the first to go to school. It was a lonely time. The teacher was kind, but very authoritarian. After the first day, she tried to protect me from their cruelty, but there were many, many incidents that she did not see, and I did not tell her about. Learning came easy for me. I quickly mastered everything she taught us. I still relish the sweet private delight I felt when she would chastise the others, "If you could only do this as well as Myrna!"

By the third grade our little school closed, and we were bused fifteen miles to the nearest town. Town school was no better. It was worse in fact, because it was bigger, and there were more children who were just as mean as the first group. The teacher was not so kind. I realized that the way to win her praise was to excel academically. It worked; and so my survive-school strategy was confirmed—figure out the teacher, figure out exactly what she wanted, and give it to her just the way she wanted it. I was at the top of the class for twelve years.

That strategy served me well through my studies in psychiatric nursing and in social work. It also worked relatively well in employment situations: identify the power, figure out what they wanted, and give it to them. I was at the top of the class.

When I was in my mid-twenties, I began a search for deeper meaning and purpose in life. I was literate. I was employable. I had a job. I was economically independent. I was a contributing member of society. I had accumulated the trappings that indicate success. But something was missing. The sense I had of myself met the criteria set out by society, but wasn't really me. I had to find my own sense of self. I decided that it was time to deal with this "bush nigger" business.

I went in search of other Indians. Having grown up in a white community, rather on the margins of a white community, with parents who assumed that assimilation was the most appropriate strategy, I did not know much about our culture, our history, our language, or our customs. I knew nothing about patterns of social interaction, attitudes, values, or world view from an Indian perspective. I had been taught none of this in school. I did know, that up until that point, being an Indian had not been a positive experience.

My search for other Indians took me to the local bars. That is where I had seen more Indian people gather than any other place. Another education. I learned about prostitution, about drugs, about how raw power and intimidation work. I learned survival skills: how to hold your liquor, how to stay out of trouble, how to wheel and deal. I was at the top of the class. And I met some wonderful friends there. It was those friends that introduced me to the people and places where I would learn about this "bush nigger" business.

A real education. The learning strategies that I had employed were not at all appropriate or effective for the education upon which I was about to embark: Indian culture and spirituality. No longer was the learning prescribed and the standards set by someone else. No longer was the learning superficial and rote. No longer could I size up the situation, determine what was wanted, and produce it, without conviction or commitment. Instead, I now had to ask, with proper reverence and ceremony, for any information or knowledge that I wanted. No one "told" me what I needed to know, I had to seek what I needed to know. No one preached and no one punished. I was accepted for being me. I was treated with respect and dignity. The sweet private delight that I had known for being at the top of the class was replaced by a deeper personal satisfaction that was rooted in honesty and respect for others and for myself. It is with some embarrassment that I remember that delight. It no longer seems proper to think of myself as being better than someone else, academically or otherwise. Since my walk on the wild side in search of "truth and wisdom," I have had several different jobs in public institutions. I have always felt the need to conform, to be tactful and not to be too "Indian." So I have in essence learned to live with one foot in each of the two worlds. It is like having one persona for the public sphere, and another for the private. The private sphere is the safest, it is where I am free to be who I am. Many of my positions have given me an opportunity to provide leadership, and if I had chosen to do so, to exercise authority and influence over others. Yet I sensed pressure from both colleagues and employers who felt that I lacked the proper academic credentials for the work I was doing. There were no complaints about the quality of my work, but a lingering kind of academic snobbery that implied that I was less than they were because I didn't have the appropriate degree. Maybe it was not the lack of a degree. Maybe it was because I am an Indian. Maybe it was because I am a woman. So, when the opportunity came, I returned to university.

Completing the first degree was drudgery. I learned some things that were useful but I realized I was slipping back into my old way of surviving school. I experienced considerable angst but in the end decided that this was a "get through it" situation, that the end was worth the means. I was able to graduate only because I could balance my sense of who I was as an Indian woman against the integrity I felt I was sacrificing. I continued on because I was committed to contributing to systemic changes in order to eliminate the oppression and exploitation of Indian people by creating opportunities and improving the situation.

I started a second degree, using the same formula—identifying the power, defining the expectations, and producing the required academic products. Then I took a class on "race and gender" and was introduced to critical pedagogy. This class brought forth the old dilemmas with new faces. First there was the original dilemma: should I just get through this, then get on with life? I did not have the time, or the energy, to "be involved" with my learning. Then were was a new face for anger: why couldn't all of my education not have been as positive and meaningful as this learning experience? Then the two thoughts converged. I felt that I had been horribly cheated. But I had no time for anger. I had glimpsed a new face for hope. The ideas contained in feminist theory and in critical theory had given me tools to make sense of the oppression and domination I had known. With that sense of hope came the sense of responsibility. I had to work to make the world a better place. But where to begin?

I see now the close relationship between racism and sexism. Prior to this learning, I believed that I had been a victim only of racism. I thought that sexism was a barrier only for white women, and I thought, that of the two "isms," racism was worse. It is now apparent that domination is domination no matter what the "grounds" and that the forces that have marginalized Indian people have also marginalized women and all those who are "other." The effect of one compounds the others.

This new understanding gave me a sense of relief. I realized that part of the "learning" I had acquired over the years was a feeling that there was something wrong with me because I was an Indian woman. Now I knew the truth. There is nothing wrong with being an Indian. There is nothing wrong with being a woman. There is nothing wrong with me. The edge is gone from my anger and I am now comfortable with the idea that individual men and individual white people are not to blame. They cannot help themselves. Capitalism and patriarchy have made them what they are. They too are waiting to be free.

The bureaucratic and capitalistic class structures which allow domination by race and the patriarchal structures which allow domination by gender have been the way of our world for such a long time that most people have come to accept the ideology and institutions of dominance without question. These assumptions "are so universally accepted they seem to be the laws of nature" (Capra cited in Rogers, 1989, p. 1). Even for women who believe they understand the dynamics of dominance and submission, it is difficult to identify all of the instances of domination and all of the situations in which our responses have been submissive. But once we start to identify them we can seek to render them less damaging.

But aggressive, confrontational strategies will not produce the kind of societal change we hope for. It will produce resistance and a further entrenchment of the ideology which informs domination. Transformation of society is likely if hegemony is transformed, slowly and carefully at the individual level. As we as individuals begin to understand feminist theory and communicate these understandings to others, pointing out androcentric biases wherever we see them, taking care to use inclusive language, assuming leadership roles wherever we can, and promoting the concepts of caring and concern, we will start to change our world. In our daily lives and in our daily teaching, we can work toward projecting our "own way of seeing social reality so successfully that (our) view is accepted as common sense and as part of the natural order" (Lewis, 1992, p. 174).

Those of us who have come to know, firsthand, the loss of self-esteem, the loss of voice and the loss of sense of person so aptly described by Sadker and Sadker (1994), must come to know, firsthand, how to make sense of our world and how to empower ourselves to make choices and changes. This requires changes in self-perception, a belief in the possibility of equity, and a redefinition of privilege. To believe that we can have the power to make choices is a significant movement in the development of our consciousness. To know that we can take a stance is a step toward gaining equality. If we assume that we are entitled to, and act in ways that suggest that we have "privilege" (Ng, 1993, p. 196), we set forth a different image of ourselves. This privilege would not adopt denial of positionalities, nor would it allow us to avoid responsibility, but it would be an image of privilege that would promote equality. For each of us, the sense, the choices, the changes, and the sequence will be different. There can be no prescriptive plan, as Magda Lewis (1992) points out, our paths to emancipation will be as diverse as we are.

By changing our personal attitudes and individual behaviors, we will not achieve equality, but that is where we must begin. Only when we have made sense of critical theory and understand equity, and only when we have positioned these ideas in our lives and in the ways we see our worlds, only then can we convey these understanding to our significant others, our families, our colleagues, and our children. Talking about equality is important. It will sharpen our perceptions, deepen our understandings, and keep the issues alive in our consciousness. If we are teachers, we can do that every day in the lives of our students. Talking about the issues will bring clarity of thought and communication which will eventually infuse our culture, and will gradually transform society until it becomes equitable and democratic.

It will be a slow process. There will continue to be resistance to change. Societal institutions and norms are all based on forms of domination, in particular, patriarchy. Patriarchy works by giving privilege and power to some adult males and promising it falsely to others (Orr, 1993, p. 24). Many males, individually and collectively, will be threatened by the challenges and will act to maintain the status quo and protect their positions of privilege. Some women, too, will resist change because they fear the loss of security, identity, and status gained through their continued submission to and association with men who, they perceive, have power and privilege (Lewis, 1992, p. 188). But I believe that change will come. As our children are released from systemic violence and the oppression of domination-based pedagogies, change will come.

I have experienced an inclusive learning environment. The contrast is immense. I only wish all of my learning could have been in such an environment. I feel somewhat like I did when I was five years old, before I went to school, before I learned that I had to be submissive in order to survive. It is ironic that with all the bitterness I have about the systemic violence of my previous schooling experiences, about having to submit to someone else's design, standards, and evaluation, now I am given the opportunity to exercise some autonomy, and I find it is daunting. I found it very difficult to write this paper, because I was given more opportunity than I had ever had in school to be in charge of my learning. Becoming emancipated could be hard work.

References

Lewis, M. (1992). Interrupting patriarchy: Politics, resistance and transformation in the feminist classroom. In C. Luke and J. Gore (Eds.), *Feminisms and critical pedagogy*. New York: Routledge.

Ng, R. (1993). A woman out of control: Deconstructing sexism and racism in the university. *Canadian Journal of Education, 18* (3), 189–205.

Orr, D. (1993). Toward a critical rethinking of feminist pedagogical praxis and resistant male students. *Canadian Journal of Education, 18* (3), 239–55.

Rogers, J. (1989). New paradigm leadership: Integrating the female ethos. *Journal of NAWDAC, 51* (4), 1–8.

Sadker, M. & Sadker, D. (1994). *Failing at fairness: How American's Schools cheat girls*. New York: Scribner's.

Chapter 13

Addressing Systemic Violence
in Education

Ailsa M. Watkinson and Juanita Ross Epp

Definition: Systemic violence is any institutionalized practice or procedure that adversely impacts on disadvantaged individuals or groups by burdening them psychologically, mentally, culturally, spiritually, economically, or physically. It includes practices and procedures that prevent students from learning, thus harming them. This may take the form of conventional policies and practices that foster a climate of violence, or policies and practices that appear neutral but result in discriminatory effects.

We have all seen the pictures in textbooks and curriculum documents—several smiling bright-eyed children with right arms raised, bursting with the correct answer, waiting to be called upon. There are a few girls, a few visible minorities, sometimes a child with a disability. The caption reads: "Our future lies in our children." This is the promise of our education system. The contributors to this book have argued that that promise is not always kept. Sometimes the girls and children of color are not called upon, and the picture disintegrates into quiet girls and marginalized minorities watching the rest perform—and empty spaces left by students who have dropped out.

As a noun, the word *promise* has three meanings, each attached to fulfillment of a commitment: the declaration, the potential, and the expectation. Because public school education is compulsory, individual members of society generally accept the promise that schooling will enhance lives. In exchange for our children's time, we are promised an education in the students'

190

best interests. The potential in that promise includes the personal fulfillment of the dreams and capabilities of individual students applied to both the private and public good. Compulsory education becomes a tragic irony when it compels students to partake in schooling in the belief that it will enhance their life chances, but in fact limits them. Schools are bound, by the promise implicit in public education, to eschew practices and policies which would detract from its fulfillment: the practices associated with systemic violence.

Violence is usually viewed in purely physical terms. In this book we have expanded the meaning of violence to include violence which interrupts the potential and the expectations of learners. Systemic violence is rarely perpetrated with intentional ill will but is built into the very essence of educational culture, and is evident in educational organization, leadership theories, and pedagogical practices. This culture exists at all levels of education: primary, secondary, and post-secondary. When students are not capable or compliant enough, the failure is shouldered by them rather than by the system. They believe themselves to be at fault and acquiesce when encouraged to exit the system with the promise unfulfilled. They rarely recognize this as a breech of the school's promise.

Not only does systemic violence inhibit personal development and the fulfillment of personal potential, it also fails society. Students whose goals and aspirations have been impeded by damaging practices in the education system do not contribute to society in the ways they might have done had the system lived up to its promise.

Reflections on Systemic Violence in Education

Each chapter of this book was written in isolation. In attempting to bring the themes together we sometimes wondered if any of them had anything to do with any of the others. What did labeling of special needs children have in common with administrative compliance? How did sexual harassment relate to gendered kindergarten play? Why did the tragedy of an isolated child remind us so much of our adult education classrooms?

But, if the topics were unrelated, why were our conclusions so similar? Somewhere in every chapter, an author called for greater understanding of those who were "other"—those whose cultural heritages, ethnic identities, gender, sexual orientation, class, experiences, or abilities differed from the "norm." Each of us asked for a re-viewing of existing practices. All of us hoped for contemplation and re-interpretation intended to reevaluate the way we viewed ourselves, our schools and our students. And each of us recognized and decried systems founded on domination.

We have argued that all students are affected by systemic violence but it is more prevalent in the lives of females, gay and lesbian students, students who are racialized, have a disability, or who are economically disadvantaged. The similarities in our work, founded on diverse stories, converged in three main areas of education. We found institutionalized systemic violence in administrative and pedagogical practices. The two were not always easy to disentangle, but by returning to the stories deconstructed throughout this book, we have attempted to identify systemic violence and suggest possible solutions.

Systemic Violence in Administrative Practice

Systemic violence in administrative practice includes any aspect of school administration that has the potential to do students harm. This includes the organizational design of educational institutions, educational leadership, and educational administrative theory. There are two types of harm. One type results from a dehumanization of students that causes them to fail, drop out, or lash out. The other arises from policies and practices that produce discriminatory effects. The dehumanizing effects come in several forms:

DEHUMANIZING EDUCATION

1. Bureaucratic educational institutions.

Most educational institutions have a "horizontal division of graded authority" (Ferguson, 1984, p. 7) which requires graded submission all the way down to the student. Bureaucracies epitomize the unequal distribution of power and dominance between men, women, and children. Learning within a de-humanized environment contributes to students' feelings of isolation and alienation (see Watkinson, chapter 1).

2. Androcentric bias in administration.

School administration is based on management literature which was written "by men for men, and its values—individualism, competition—define success in a masculine way" (Brandt, 1992, p. 47). Male-dominated family structures and patriarchal organizational settings reinforce each other (Morgan, 1986). Most schools are still managed by men, but as we have argued in several chapters (Epp, Watkinson, Ho, Webb and Hughson, Tite, and Richards), female administrative styles are likely to change many aspects of leadership.

3. Militarism of educational administration theory.

The intent of schools, to foster a learning environment that enhances personal potential, is not the same as the intent of military training, which is to provide a predictable "human factor" during times of conflict and aggression. Unfortunately, military theories and tactics have infiltrated educational practices (Noble, 1988, p. 241; see also Watkinson, chapter 1).

4. The inherent violence of "discipline."

By punishing children "for their own good" (Miller, 1990), we destroy their sense of self and their innate belief in their own worth. Punishment destroys the child's mechanism for understanding that violence is wrong. This also serves to prevent teachers from carrying out their professional duty to apprehend physical abuse and distinguish it from appropriate discipline (see Tite in chapter 3).

The administrative dehumanizing of students is dangerous to all children but is even more harmful to children who are "other." We have used this term throughout the book to describe students who are different from the perceived norm in terms of color, sexual preference, religion, ability, intellect, body size, language, gender, and class (Ellsworth, 1994). These categories include a majority of students. This majority is harmed by a discriminatory school culture that does not notice or ignores the social, historical, legal, and economic differences among students. Some examples:

DISCRIMINATORY SCHOOL CULTURE

1. Inhospitable school culture.

A large percent of dropouts are members of minorities, lesbians, gay men, and the poor (Fine, 1991). The impersonal environment that is characteristic of large educational bureaucracies eclipses the circumstances of particular students rendering them invisible. Thus students from diverse backgrounds "are, on average, performing somewhat worse than students from other communities" (Begin and Caplan, 1994, p. 44). As Cummins notes, "students who have the most difficulty in schools are those who have experienced a long history of discrimination and prejudice" (Cummins, 1989, p. 8).

2. Labeling individuals.

The process of identifying, categorizing, and labeling is a practice of convenience and utility which blinds educators to the needs of the individual. Labels take living subjects and turn them into objects of scrutiny (see Monteath and Cooper in chapter 7).

3. Treating all individuals the same.

School expectations that require all students to follow the same pattern discriminate against individuals who are unable to conform. Notions of fairness in which, in order to be fair, all students are treated the same, may not be all that "fair." Monteath and Cooper (chapter 7), point out the negative affects of uniform expectations on special needs students. Similar isolation results if students have been abused (Tite, chapter 3), lack English skills

(Wason-Ellam, chapter 5; Ho, chapter 11), are not white (Ndunda, chapter 6), or have discipline problems (Webb, chapter 11).

4. Failing to address abuse.

Statistics show that 33 percent to 50 percent of children have been sexually abused (Bagley 1991, pp. 103–4) and even more are victims of physical abuse. As Tite (chapter 3) has pointed out, children may be in need of intervention in cases of abuse but teachers may be reluctant to report it. Teachers focused on intellectual development and the importance of discipline may be unable to identify abused children. But teacher responsibility goes beyond reporting because they are in a position to help children understand what abuse is. Sometimes children are unaware that what is happening to them is abuse. Brookes (1992), is especially critical of school structures which make it unlikely that a child will recognize abuse, and name it as such thus making it impossible for a child to access the system in order to get help.

5. Harassment which is tolerated and named at peril.

Power differentials make harassment possible and deter those who would identify it and seek to correct it. The harassed may be accused of weaknesses and aberrant behavior. Richards (chapter 9) described an instance in which a teacher was blamed for her own harassment because of the administrator's belief in a confluence of the desexualized norm of mother/teacherhood and the innocence of childhood "pranks." Warren (chapter 10) reiterated a case in which the administration blamed faculty members for identifying a harasser rather than letting blame fall on the harasser himself. In both cases, those naming the harassment were identified as "aberrent" rather than the harassing behavior.

All of these issues, particularly the automatic questioning of the integrity of persons reporting behaviors that they feel are not just, make it difficult for anyone to question the already obscured rituals and accepted traditions associated with educational administration. In our work we have advocated a re-examination of "common sense" administrative practices.

Systemic Violence of Pedagogical Practice

Pedagogy is "the integration in practice of particular curriculum content and design, classroom strategies and techniques, and evaluation, purpose and method" (Rogers cited in McLaren, 1989, p. 161). It includes everything that teachers do. Systemic violence of pedagogical practice is not purposeful damage; teachers do not teach with the intent of marginalizing students or causing them harm. They are working in a traditional paradigm, using many practices that, on the surface, are productive. But student learning can be harmed by curriculum content—what it contains, what it leaves out or how it is interpreted, classroom design, classroom strategies, evaluations, interactions, and teaching methods. When these practices are examined problematically they can be identified as sytemically violent in that they prevent some students from learning. Pedagogy has the potential to damage children in several ways:

1. Pedagogy as social control.

As mentioned in chapter 1 (Watkinson), traditional pedagogy regards the student as a passive learner in need of schooling by an authority. A student's inherent dignity is denied unless the student can demonstrate her or his worth by providing evidence of acculturation, deference to power, and acceptance of epistemic absolutes. For the un-acculturated, "the school has its own arsenal of coercive weaponry—suspension, verbal abuse, corporal punishment, withholding of affection, denial of 'privileges' (recess, athletics, bathroom), and above all else, the dreaded lower grade, or 'bad' reference" (Purpel, 1989, p. 47). The violence of indoctrination is social control rather than liberation and empowerment.

2. Pedagogy that marginalizes.

Traditional pedagogy seeks harmony and avoids conflict. To do this it must perpetuate the "colonizing fantasy" (hooks, 1994) that we are a monolithic people with similar needs and abilities. Traditional pedagogical methods are more individualistic and competitive, and advantage students with a white middle-class background, and those whose first language is English. Teaching methods based on rote learning give primacy to the cognitive domain and avoid the affective. Pedagogical practices which pay little or no attention to the affective domain may appear to be harmonious, in that there is no controversial discourse, but they do not reflect or consider the diverse needs and concerns of students (see Ndunda in chapter 6).

Marginalization results in the silencing of those who are "other." Ndunda (chapter 6) described her own withdrawal from classroom discussions, not because others told her she must not speak but because she felt compelled to minimize her difference. Azur (Ho, chapter 11), a poet in her homeland, had no access to poetry and was forced into silence by a system that assumed that those who did not speak English were less capable and could not be expected to contribute anything worthwhile. Duc Lan (Wason-Ellam, chapter 5) was so marginalized by lack of language that his best friends were video game characters. Schooling using traditional methods did nothing to alleviate the exclusion. In chapter 1 (Watkinson) a teacher was unable to see the inherent exclusion in the practice of reciting the Lord's Prayer and in chapter 7 (Rossler), an aboriginal student displaying unusual behavior was ignored in the assumption that such behavior was "normal" to those of her race. The "common sense" exclusion of those who are "other" (Ng, 1993) was accepted even by those who were excluded.

3. Monolithic curriculum

"Objectivity" and the restrictive codes that forbid personal discourse contribute to an understanding of what is considered "academic." The positivistic approach to understanding what is "knowledge" excludes the lives, realities, and perceptions of many students. Only those with authority and attainment are considered sources of "knowledge." If the students' experiences do not coincide with the authority's interpretation of knowledge, students can only assume that what they know is meaningless and worthless. The "common sense" of the exclusion is reinforced (see Ho, Webb, and Hughson, chapter 11).

4. The assumption of the naturalness of childhood.

Common sense also invites us to believe in the inherent innocence of children. In chapter 9, Richards examined how that assumption results in an administrative culture which allows students to sexually harass teachers with impunity. The assumption that play is natural and should not be interrupted also results in the early establishment of domination and submission. In chapter 4, Whitty described an intervention process in which the teacher was able to arrest the domination, and acceptance of domination, in a kindergarten classroom. Games and play are preparation for life and it is through them that children try out what they will become. Lack of intervention in "natural" play allows children to learn exclusion as subtly as they learn language (Rizvi, 1993).

Central to systemic violence in pedagogy is the exclusion of students who are different. These students are prevented, by that exclusion, from making positive contributions to society. The violence of pedagogy is considered "normal" and is supported by administrative practice. The two complement each other to the extent that they are often indistinguishable.

The systemic violence evident in administrative and pedagogical practice share another common feature: they are both applied by people to everyday situations and the cycle that perpetuates them can only be broken by people. The basis for addressing systemic violence in both administrative and pedagogical practice lies in personal responses to elicit change.

Addressing Systemic Violence

Systemic violence in administrative and pedagogical practices are endemic to schools and are often carried out through unreflective repetition of age-old practices. They are not done to inflict intentional harm and, in most instances, the people responsible would claim that what they have done was in the students' best interests. These practices are legal, time-honored, and expected. They reflect the "common sense," taken-for-granted administrative and pedagogical practices designed, in large part, for the education of a homogeneous group of children with a common ancestry. We have used Gramsci's definition of "common sense" to draw attention to normal and ordinary actions and practices whose banality renders them, and the damage that they do, invisible (Ng, 1993, p. 52).

These practices, however unintentional and systemically validated, are carried out and reinforced by individuals working within the educational culture. By apprising educators of systemic violence, its forms and effects, we can interrupt it. As Bannerji states, "It is entirely possible to be critical of racism at the level of ideology, politics and institutions . . . yet possess a great quantity of common sense racism" (1987, p. 10). And as Watkinson said in chapter 1, "It is also entirely possible to teach tolerance yet possess a great quantity of common sense intolerance."

In what follows, we will attempt to identify some starting points for addressing systemic violence in both administrative and pedagogical practice. Our proposals for change constitute an "affirmative action plan." We use the term to mean a holistic, concerted, and coordinated effort to change the "status quo," and affirm the differences among us.

Although we have identified discrete aspects of systemic violence, attempts to address it require holistic forms of intervention. For example, harassment is violence that could be addressed in several related ways. It could be controlled by the application of administrative policies that would address the issue, and by the use of pedagogical practice that would allow students to understand the relationship between harassment and dominance. It could be made real through personal interventions intended to affirm victims and to help perpetrators understand their own behavior.

Child abuse is similar. Administrative structures could be enforced to ensure that students are protected through legal structures and formal protocol. Pedagogy could be reflective and connective, thus enabling children to understand the affective and apply this learning in their own lives. All of this would require personal intervention, understanding, and awareness from individual teachers.

The list goes on. Abuse of women by men is founded on the abuse of girls by boys. Kindergarten exclusion, if unchecked, leads little boys to believe that they can claim spatial privilege and little girls to believe that they must accept submissive roles. Administrative structures can be put in place to ensure equality for girls and boys but they must be backed by pedagogical practice and personal commitment before students will truly believe the equity message. We advocate the following integrated means of beginning to address systemic violence in both administrative and pedagogical practice. All of them would require intervention at the personal level by individuals in all educational roles. The suggestions for change which follow are written in the tense of promise:

1. *A humane learning environment.* Our humanistic school setting is characterized by the "ethic of care" (Gilligan, 1982) which values connection and is concerned with problems of detachment, abandonment, and indifference. A humanistic school setting is a student-centered environment with small classes, student input in decision making and attention to individual needs. The idea that bigger schools are better has been rejected in favor of smaller school populations. In such an atmosphere, students and teachers know each other well and work cooperatively to nurture "fundamental, humane and creative educational thinking" (Amonashvili, 1989, p. 585). A nurturing, positive and supportive environment promotes social connectedness, cooperative behavior and creative and self-enhancing independence (Schultz, 1987, p. 32). Violent acts diminish within an environment of familiarity and connectedness. The interconnectedness and familiarity produce "a world of caring where no one is left alone or hurt" (Gilligan, 1982, p. 62). The humane learning environment has no walls. The former "outside community" dissolved into the community of learning, creating a symbiotic learning environment—and a welcoming environment for all parents and community members.

2. *Modeling equality.* We have changed our metaphor of schools from organizations to communities, and our metaphor of chief education officer to community developer, educational care giver, or educational facilitator. The selection of educators is based on the credential of "caring," that is, the demonstrated characteristic of the educator's capacity for compassion. In addition, the meritorious qualifications in the hiring process include previously marginalizing characteristics such as cultural heritage, ethnic identity, gender, class experience, or sexual orientation. Previously excluded knowledge, experience, interpretation, and perspective are valued and their development is encouraged. The inclusion of

previously racialized and marginalized teachers and administrators reflects the diversity among the learners.

A small step in modeling equality is achieved when we, the teachers, practice some of the principles basic to critical pedagogy by reflecting upon and identifying our own biases. Together teachers and students examine the classroom for bias, discuss the implications, and consciously aim to use inclusive practices. Students learn that there are socially constricted groups of the "privileged" and the "other," and they learn that sexism, racism, and classism are not normal. The critical examination of all aspects of life—the processes, situations, and circumstances encountered on a daily basis—helps students recognize imbalance in the distribution of privilege. Students examine their dominance and submission roles. By disrupting the traditional patterns in the schools we are dismantling support from existing structures. We do not expect students to understand and challenge domination and subservience if we, as their models, demonstrate submission, hatred, contempt, and callousness.

3. *Mutual respect.* When identifying special needs and individual differences, we do not lose sight of the person. Identification of special needs does not mean stigmatization since stigmatization only makes dealing with difference more difficult. Adherence to a belief in a "norm" means that all who do not meet that "norm" are deficient. Differences do not have a value attached but provide a learning opportunity for all. The "norm" includes a diverse range of students, all of whom are expected to contribute to classroom discourse. All "stories of experience" are positive contributions to the curriculum (Monteath and Cooper, chapter 7).

As Whitty (chapter 4), has pointed out, ensuring mutuality requires the questioning of daily routines and consideration of the choices that students make in the classroom. Who is choosing what, when, where, with whom, and under what circumstances? Spatial dominance is addressed by classroom dialogue, questioning of practice and re-organization of space. Teachers who speak directly with the children about choices, challenge societal expectations, and help students do the same.

4. *Inclusive pedagogy.* Inclusive pedagogy is characterized by a belief in the importance of the affective and a conviction that true education must include recognition and analysis of dominance and

submission. It places emphasis on the importance of emotions, feelings, and personal responses. The lack of the affective in our schools teaches children to mask their feelings and disown their emotions (Brookes, 1992).

The curriculum is reconstructed from the "standpoint of the least advantaged" (Connell, 1993; also Watkinson, Epp and Ndunda in this book). This is possible through participatory democracy, and the valuing of student direction in decision making and curriculum planning.

Inclusive curriculum necessitates the asking of questions which may bring discomfort and in some cases, disharmony, such as: Who decides curriculum? Who is left out? Whose ideology is represented here? Would this have the same meaning if examined by people not of our culture? The questioning provides classroom space where educators/teachers and students raise critical questions and interrogate texts as cultural texts in light of their experiences (Ndunda, chapter 6). As Richards (chapter 9) suggested, by using a poststructural analysis, we chip away at supposed truths by opening up a competing discursive space that destabilizes the debilitating effects of dominant discourses. We make space for the stories and histories of all children, we encourage them to celebrate their culture, ethnicity, and heritage.

The techniques used in inclusive pedagogy are important but so too is the provision of a risk-free environment in which half-formulated questions and thoughts can be aired, accepted, and honed into meaning without fear of derision. As Freire (1970) has advocated, in "liberating pedagogy" content is secondary to dialogue—with students and teachers "together seeking reality" (p. 33).

5. *Naming abuse.* Corporal punishment was one of the most difficult pedagogical traditions to challenge. It was accepted as a necessary part of child raising and student discipline. As we have seen (Tite, chapter 3), educators had difficulty defining it as abusive so they are reluctant to name it as such. Within a school environment focused on caring, connectedness, and community, there is no place for the abuse of students in the name of discipline.

Part of the reluctance of teachers and administrators to give up corporal punishment was based on a belief that children cannot be "controlled" by other means. In order to understand troublesome and troubled students, we attempt to understand the connection between unmet personal needs, the use of authority, and its undertones of violence. Teachers who have chosen not to use authoritative methods have been able to "control" their classrooms for years. These teachers have learned to use inclusive problem-solving approaches, respect, humor, understanding, and inventiveness, to win over unruly students (Epp, chapter 2).

Teachers are working at understanding their own role in addressing child abuse when it is perpetrated by other adults. Students who have been abused are given an ear and a voice. The silencing of abused children (and adults) deprived them of avenues through which to address their abuse and by which to heal the hurt. It was not only the abuse, but also the lack of attention to it, that damaged children and robbed them of a fulfilled adult life. Schools do not ignore the abused among them.

Abuse is the personification of dominance. It is addressed in the schools through identification of both the crimes themselves and the students who have been hurt. Educators teach children what they should be able to expect from adult caregivers and provide avenues to help and protect children who are not receiving adequate care. Teachers do two things: they help students to identify and grapple with their hurt and they provide protection and ongoing support for children at risk.

Addressing systemic violence was no simple matter. It required challenges to many traditionally accepted "common sense" practices in both administrative and pedagogical practice. But as a result of our collective efforts we now have a humane learning environment in which educators model equity and mutual respect, use inclusive pedagogy, and provide a risk-free environment in which students can question conventional practice and wisdom.

In Closing

Eradicating systemic violence in education requires changes at every level of education and the affirmative commitment of all school personnel. In order for us to address school violence, we need to re-think education: its purpose, its delivery, its structure, its staffing, its content, its leadership, its promise. Individuals can begin the process and build toward the development of a "critical mass." The re-forming of school structures and culture can best be realized through a collective process. The contributors to this book are an example of just that. We began by developing our concerns and ideas as individuals and found resonance in the collection of our thoughts and the thoughts of the collective. The transformation from one person to a critical mass is this book.

Each of us has contributed to the identification of systemic violence in education and the identification of possible solutions to overcome its insidious effects. By doing so we believe we are on the road to the promise of education, one that is committed to upholding the dignity and enhancing the potential aspirations and dreams of all those who learn and work in the educational community.

References

Anonashvili, S. (1989). Non-directive teaching and the humanization of the educational process. *Prospects, 19*.

Bagley, C. (1991). The prevalence and mental health sequels of child sexual abuse in a community sample of women aged 18 to 27. *Canadian Journal of Community Mental Health, 10* (1), 103–104.

Bannerji, H. (1987). Introducing racism: Notes towards an anti-racist feminism. *Resources for Feminist Research, 16*, 10.

Begin, M. and Caplan, G. (1994). *For the love of learning: Report of the Royal Commission on Learning.* Toronto: Queen's Printer for Ontario.

Brandt, R. (1992). On rethinking leadership: A conversation with Tom Sergiovanni. *Educational Leadership, 49* (5).

Brookes, L. A. (1992). *Feminist pedagogy: An autobiographical approach.* Halifax: Fernwood

Connell, R. W. (1993) *Schools and social justice.* Montreal: Our Schools Our Selves.

Cummins, J. (1989). *Empowering minority students.* California: California Association of Bilingual Education.

Ellsworth, E. (1994). Why doesn't this feel empowering? Working through the repressive myths of critical pedagogy. In L. Stone (Ed.), *The education feminism reader*. New York: Routledge.

Ferguson, K. (1984). *The feminist case against bureaucracy*. Philadelphia: Temple University Press.

Fine, M. (1991). *Framing dropouts: Notes on the politics of an urban public high school*. Albany, New York: State University of New York Press.

Freire, P. (1970). *Pedagogy of the oppressed*. Translated by M. B. Ramos. New York: The Seabury Press.

Gilligan, C. (1982). *In a different voice: Psychological theory and women's development*. Cambridge: Harvard University Press.

hooks, b. (1994). *Teaching to transgress: Education as the practice of freedom*. New York: Routledge Press.

Martin, J. (1993). *Changing the educational landscape*. New York: Routledge Press.

McLaren, P. (1989). *Life in school: An introduction to critical pedagogy in the foundations of education*. New York: Longman.

Miller, A. (1990). *For your own good*. New York: Doubleday Press.

Morgan, G. (1989). *Images of Organizations*. London: Sage.

Ng, R. (1993). Racism, sexism, and nation building in Canada. In C. McCarthy and W. Crichlow (Eds.), *Race, identity, and representation in education* (p. 52). New York: Routledge.

Noble, D. D. (1988). Education, technology and the military. In L. E. Beyer and M. W. Apple (Eds.), *The Curriculum: Problems, Politics, and Possibilities* (p. 241). New York: State University of New York Press.

Noddings, N. (1992). *The challenge to care in schools*. New York: Teachers College.

Purpel, D. E. (1989). *The moral and spiritual crisis in education: A curriculum for justice and compassion in education*. Massachusetts: Bergin & Garvey.

Rizvi, F. (1993). Children and the grammar of popular racism. In McCarthy, C. and Critchlow, W. (Eds.), *Race, identity and representation in education* (pp. 126–139). New York: Routledge.

Sadker, M. and Sadker, D. (1994). *Failing at fairness: How American schools cheat girls*. New York: Scribner's.

Schultz, E. W. et al. (1987). School climate: Psychological health and well being in school. *Journal of School Health, 57.*

Sergiovanni, T. J. (1992). Why we should seek substitutes for leadership. *Educational Leadership, 49* (5), 41.

Sergiovanni, T. J. (1994). *Building community in schools.* San Francisco: Jossey Bass.

Shakeshaft, C. (1989). *Women in educational administration.* Newbury Park: Sage.

Watkinson, A. M. (1993, June) . *Inequality and or hormones.* Paper presented at the meeting of the Canadian Association for the Study of Educational Administration, Ottawa, ON.

Watkinson, A. M. (1994). Equality, empathy and the administration of education. *Education and Law Journal, 5* (3) 273–304.

Watkinson, A. M. (1995a). Hostile lessons: Sexual harassment in schools. *The Canadian Administrator 34* (1), 1–12.

Watkinson, A. M. (1995b). Valuing women educators. In S. M. Natale and B. M. Rothschild (Eds.), *Values, work, education: The meanings of work* (pp. 107–30). Atlanta: Rodopi.

Contributors

Karyn Cooper is a Ph.D. student at the University of Alberta. Her doctoral dissertation examines and challenges the distinction that our culture makes between the self-identity of child and adult learners using a phenomenological, existential, and narrative approach to inquiry in education. She has worked extensively with "special needs" and "at risk" children, especially those who have difficulties in language learning. Karyn has taught reading at the elementary school level and principles of reading instruction at the graduate level. In her life and in her work, she is deeply committed to issues of personal and cultural change. She hopes for the creation of humane learning environments that respect children's affective capacities while stretching their cognitive abilities.

Juanita Ross Epp began her career as a teacher and spent fifteen years teaching at both the elementary and secondary levels. Her Ph.D. is in Educational Administration from the University of Saskatchewan. She now teaches at Lakehead University in Ontario, Canada. Although she has tried to focus on administration in her research, she often strays into issues of gender and pedagogy as is evident in her publications in journals such as the *Educational Administration Quarterly*, *The Journal of Higher Education*, and *The NASSP Bulletin*.

Laura Ho works as a teacher, counselor, researcher, and teacher/educator and concerns herself with schooling for children and adults in a multicultural community. Her doctoral research, completed in 1993, concerns the experience of immigrants in

Canadian adult education. She is currently the director of Community Cultures Institute in Edmonton, Alberta.

Elizabeth Anne Hughson is a chartered psychologist with a background in Clinical Psychology and Rehabilitation/Disabilities Studies; an associate professor in the Rehabilitation Studies Programme, Department of Educational Psychology, University of Calgary; and a consultant to the Behaviour Support Team, an outreach service available to adults and children of families with developmental disabilities. As a Ph.D. candidate (Interdisciplinary Studies) at the University of Alberta, her dissertation research focuses on the meaning of safety for women surviving abuse from an intimate partner. Anne's publications and research interests include issues of power and devaluation, program evaluation, intervention approaches in community-based services, and inclusive educational practices for people with disabilities.

Lisa Jadwin teaches in the English Department at St. John Fisher College. She has published essays on pedagogical theory and on Victorian and contemporary literature. She has just completed a book on cognition and writing development and is currently coauthoring a study of the works of Charlotte Brontë (Twayne, 1997).

Sandra Monteath is a writer who holds a masters in Environmental Studies from York University and a Ph.D. in Education (Sociology of Education) from the University of Toronto. She once taught art and English at the secondary school level and spent many years as an editor in educational and academic publishing. She has also designed educational games. Sandra's mode of inquiry is at once analytic and ethnographic, and she writes from an embodied, feminist standpoint. Currently she is working on a children's book on Arya Tara, a Buddha who vowed always to appear in female form, and is also completing a study, "No strangers to sorrow: Conversations with children about suffering," on children's understanding of, and talk about suffering.

Mutindi Ndunda was born, raised and partly schooled in Uvuuni village, Kilome Division, Makueni District, Kenya. She was brought up in a "modern" polygamous home. She graduated with a

B.Ed. (Science) degree from Nairobi University in 1983 and taught mathematics and chemistry at the high school level from 1983 to 1988. In 1988 she was awarded a scholarship to pursue a master's degree in Canada and graduated with a master's degree in Curriculum and Instruction in 1990. Her dissertation examined girls' experiences of science education. She completed a Ph.D. in Social Foundations of Educational Policy at the University of British Columbia in August 1995.

Elisabeth Richards is a doctoral student in the Department of Sociology at the Ontario Institute for Studies in Education. As a former Core French teacher who has taught French at both the elementary and secondary level in the Ontario public school system, she continues to be interested in issues pertaining to second language instruction. Her dissertation will be a study of French teachers' experiences in staff meetings.

Linda Rossler began her teaching career in early childhood education and went on to become a special educator, vice principal, principal, and assistant superintendent. Her experience includes teaching in both elementary and high school settings in rural and urban locations. Linda holds a B.Ed. in early childhood education, an M.Ed. in curriculum and instruction, and a Ph.D. in educational administration.

Rosonna Tite is an Associate Professor in the Faculty of Education at Memorial University of Newfoundland. Besides teaching sociology of education in the teacher education program and policy studies at the graduate level, she is coordinator of the Women's Studies Graduate Program. Currently, Rosonna is collaborating with the Newfoundland A Capella Network in a project aimed at using dramatic fiction to engage junior high students in thinking about issues of violence.

Catharine E. Warren is an adult educator and professor at the University of Calgary. She holds a Ph.D. in Sociology from the University of London, England, and has a special interest in gender issues. She taught secondary school science for six years. Her book on immigrant women, *Vignettes of life: Experiences of New Cana-*

dian Women (Detselig, 1986) won honorable mention in the non-fiction category at the Alberta Culture Book Awards.

Linda Wason-Ellam is an ethnographer who researches the "social lives of children in cross-cultural literacy classrooms." She is a professor at the University of Saskatchewan teaching courses in Reading, Language Arts, and Children's Literature. A former teacher and consultant, she has published many articles in educational journals and is the author of the following books: *Start with a Story, Literacy Moments to Report Cards, Sharing Stories with Children*, and coauthor of *Horizons in Literacy*. Her forthcoming book addresses teaching and learning in cross-cultural classrooms.

Ailsa M. Watkinson is a researcher and equality consultant with a special interest in the area of education and human rights laws. She received her Ph.D. in educational administration from the University of Saskatchewan in 1992. Prior to returning to the university in 1989, she worked for twelve years with the Saskatchewan Human Rights Commission. In 1987, Ailsa received a national award from the Canadian Association for the Study of Educational Administration for her master's thesis entitled *Student Discipline and the Canadian Charter of Rights and Freedoms*. She is currently writing a book about student rights and human rights law in Canada. Her book is scheduled for publication in 1997.

Kathie Webb completed her doctorate in Educational Policy Studies at the University of Alberta in the fall of 1995, funded by a Canadian Commonwealth Ph.D. Scholarship. Her dissertation focused on teachers' personal practical knowledge and the implications for curriculum change and teacher development. Before coming to Canada in 1991, Kathie taught grades 7–12 for seventeen years in New South Wales, Australia and was a department head in a large high school. Her interest in systemic violence in education stems from her experiences as a teacher, graduate student, and educational researcher. She has chapters in *Researching Educational Administration and Leadership in Canadian Education* (Detselig, 1995) and has two coauthored papers in *Recreating relationships: Collaboration and educational reform* (in press, H. Christiansen et al., eds., SUNY Press). She has also published in *Teacher Research:*

The Journal of Classroom Inquiry, The Journal of Educational Thought and *Teaching and Teacher Education.*

Pam Whitty teaches early childhood and curriculum theory courses at the University of New Brunswick in Fredericton (UNBF). Prior to her appointment to UNBF in 1991, she taught kindergarten, first grade, and special education over a twelve-year period. In her academic work she continues to reclaim the educational thought of Helen Keller.

Myrna Yuzicapi started her career in Psychiatric Nursing, but most of her career has been in the field of Indian Education. She is a former director of the Saskatchewan Indian Cultural College, was the founding director of the Indian Social Work Education program, and coordinated the establishment of the Joe Duquette High School (formerly the Saskatoon Native Survival School) an all-Native school in Saskatoon. For the past ten years Myrna has been employed as a counsellor at SIAST Kelsey Institute in Saskatoon. She holds a Diploma in Psychiatric Nursing, a Bachelor of Education (U of S) and a post-graduate diploma in Education Administration (U of S). She plans to complete the requirements for her Master's degree in the next year.

Index*

Abir-Am, P. G. & Outram, D., 98, 108
Abrahams, N., Casey, K., & Daro, D.,
    37, 53
abuse, child: 37–53; 195; assumptions
    about, 38; based in biased values,
    38, 44; breaking the cycle of, 28;
    criminals as products of, 26–27; de-
    fined, 40; difficulties in detecting,
    38, 45; discipline as, 46; emotional,
    40; gendered responses to, 29,
    42–43; 50; neglect, 40; pornog-
    raphy as, 41; reporting, 40–43,
    50–51, 48; sexual and physical,
    11, 37
abuse: as personification of domi-
    nance, 203; corporal punishment as,
    26, 45, 202; naming, 202–03; of
    power, xiv; of teachers, 141; spousal,
    170–173; institutional, 34
access to play area by gender, 62–65
administrative harassing behavior,
    151; controlling techniques, 166
administrators: as change agents, 34;
    as oppressors, 3; men as "naturals,"

33; separated from teacher roles,
    32–33; women as, 32–35
adultcentric observer, 76
affective: domain, 197; needs, 29
alienation, 26, 95
Amonashvili, S., 17, 20, 200, 204
androcentric bias in administration,
    8–9, 193
Aronowitz, S., 7, 20
Attias, R., & Goodwin, J., 50, 54
authority: and harassment, 155–56;
    and patriarchal assumptions, 154; as
    "power over," 25; as pedagogy, 29;
    covert of women, 148; decentering
    of, 132; feminist, 29; in families, 33;
    in student centered classrooms,
    130, 132–33; linked to obedience,
    25; "natural," of men, 33; of women
    teachers, 133

bad girls, 166–67; and "safety" of mar-
    riage, 172; behavior linked to acade-
    mics, 176
Bagley, C. 11, 20, 195, 204

*This book contains many personal stories which are listed together under "narratives" rather
    than by individual names or topics.

213